THE
DREAM
WORKBOOK

THE DREAM WORKBOOK

Simple

exercises

to unravel

the secrets

of your

dreams

ROBERT LANGS, M.D.

Alliance Publishing, Inc.
Brooklyn, New York

ISBN 0-9641509-1-3

Book design by Suzanne H. Holt
Produced by Publisher's Studio, Albany, New York

Alliance books are available
at special discounts for bulk purchases for sales promotions,
premiums, fund-raising, or educational use.
For details, contact:

Alliance Publishing, Inc.
P.O. Box 080377
Brooklyn, New York 11208-0002

Distributed to the trade by National Book Network, Inc.

10 8 6 4 2   3 5 7 9

Contents

Part I

DREAMS, STORIES, AND TRIGGERS

Chapter 1

Wisdom Through Dreams

This book is a journey that will take you into the deepest reaches of the human mind. It is a voyage into the mysterious and marvelous underworld that our dreams so cleverly describe and define, a world also reflected in the myriad of stories and tales we dream up and tell ourselves and others, almost unnoticed, day in and day out.

There are vast and valuable secrets buried deep within all storied communications, which can be gleaned only through a decoding process called *trigger decoding*—a way of unraveling the mysteries of dreams in light of the events or triggers to which they are a response. Trigger decoding takes you into a realm of experience and knowledge that no other way of working with dreams makes available to you. It is a unique method that takes you into a special and important part of your mind as it endeavors to cope with life's vicissitudes.

Developing the skills that will enable you to trigger decode your own dreams can make a significant difference in nearly every aspect of your life. It is my intention to show you how to find your way through the mental maze you must negotiate in order to reach into the deepest strata and meanings of your dreams and stories. Together, we will travel to the place in your own mind where you can discover and make use of the remarkably profound and otherwise inaccessible wisdom you happen to possess. And while the journey will be filled with twists and turns, it will be well worth the taking.

DREAMS AND STORIES

The chariot we will use to reach this compelling and marvelous netherworld is built on four wheels. The first two wheels are similar in design and structure. They are the aforementioned *dreams* and *stories.*

Both dreams and stories are carriers of the *encoded messages* we need to decode to reach our destination. Every communication with a storied line—from tall tales to short dreams—is an entry point into the depths of our minds. They take us to a place outside of the range of awareness where we struggle unconsciously, much as we do consciously, to cope with reality and life itself.

Stories are inherently layered with meaning. A portion of that meaning is out in the open, up front, and etched into the surface (manifest) story as told. A rose is a rose is a rose—a simple message with perhaps a few implications, but nothing more.

However, some of the meaning contained in every story is not at all apparent on the surface. These meanings are disguised in the very same images that give the tale its direct meanings.

> *All stories have two distinctive meanings at the same time—one direct (conscious) and the other camouflaged or encoded (unconscious).*

The human mind is able to use language so that we can say one thing and mean it, while saying another thing in disguise and mean that too. This is one of the least appreciated miracles of human language and communication: our ability to send two messages with one narrative missile.

What makes this story-telling faculty so important is that nature has seen to it that, when it comes to emotional concerns, *our greatest and most remarkable intelligence operates outside of awareness*. We are quite able to process and adapt to emotionally charged issues both consciously and unconsciously. We have two minds to get us through life.

The results of our efforts at *unconscious* processing are surprisingly incisive and they are reported to the outer world—to ourselves and others—through *storied messages*. But these results are not to be found in the direct or surface story of a dream, but in a latent story that is camouflaged or encoded into the dream images.

We are all great narrators, story tellers, and dreamers. Instinctively we reveal in *disguise* the workings of our unconscious minds as they operate, remarkably enough, without awareness—and always as part of our efforts to cope with life's stresses and strains.

> *Therefore, dreams and stories are the means through which we enter the powerful world of unconscious experience.*

THE DESIGN OF THE MIND

The third wheel of this chariot has been built from new insights into the human mind. Dreams and stories are fashioned by a special part of our mind—the part of the mind that has evolved to cope unconsciously with everything we experience that has even a modicum of emotional power. This refers, of course, to just about everything in life that counts for anything. Having a grasp of the design of the mind will give us a workable framework for understanding and learning the details of the dream decoding process which will soon occupy our attention.

The human mind is fashioned in an unusual and surprising way for emotional coping.

> *Emotional issues are so complex and potentially disturbing that we have not one but two systems of the mind in order to deal with them.*

When it comes to dealing with the practical problems and exigencies of everyday life—meeting our basic responsibilities and handling the necessities of survival—we cope with the relevant issues with a single system of the mind. Quite naturally, this system is connected to awareness—to get through each day we need to know exactly what we're dealing with, how we're responding, and how well we are doing. In that way, we can make any necessary adjustments and, in general, be successful in our quests.

The conscious world—the one we're directly aware of—is such that what we see and hear must be straightforward. Conscious messages also must be direct and manifest so we can grasp them immediately and without confusion—our lives depend on this. These operations are carried out by the system of the mind we call the *conscious system* because it operates mainly in the realm of awareness.

When it comes to emotionally charged issues and experiences, the situation gets more complicated. We do, of course, try to cope with emotional concerns directly and consciously, but emotional issues overtax the conscious mind. We don't function very well on our jobs or as parents or spouses when we are worried about someone or something that has hurt and upset us. We're distracted and far from our best.

To enhance survival, then, evolution has favored minds that can keep the conscious system's survival efforts in peak condition. And this is done by automatically bypassing awareness when we experience potentially disruptive emotional impingements.

We have the faculty of receiving emotionally charged inputs unconsciously and of processing them unconsciously as well.

This means that many of the most important aspects of our emotional lives are experienced outside of awareness— and are dealt with or adapted to without our knowing it as well.

Unconscious experience and coping are part of the activities of the second system of our minds: *the deep unconscious system.* The inputs into this system, and the ways in which the system processes or deals with them, are unseen, but critical to emotional life. Remarkably, unconscious processing also is far superior to conscious processing—in the emotional domain, unconscious wisdom far exceeds conscious wisdom. In this light, you can see why getting in touch with these unconscious processes is so important and enlightening.

The main way we reach into this unconscious world is through the encoded messages the unconscious system emits through narratives and stories—dreams and otherwise. But in order to comprehend these messages, we must know what they are a response to—the stimuli, input, or *triggers* that activate the system. Decoding disguised messages from the unconscious mind in light of the triggers that set that part of the mind into action is called *trigger decoding.* It is a method of unraveling unconscious messages which is based on the realization that the unconscious mind is a coping system; in order to understand its disguised messages, we must know what the system is trying to cope with.

Strangely enough, then, we are at our wisest in the world of emotions when we have no idea what we're experiencing and thinking. The design of the mind is quite peculiar; most of the power over our lives exists in a subterranean mental chamber hidden from view and seen only through intense camouflage. This means that our use of psychological defenses and our ways of keeping important perceptions and thoughts outside of awareness are not only based on early traumas and early and later conflicts, but are also inherent to the evolved design of the mind.

To carry out trigger decoding, then, you need to be prepared to face your hidden conflicts, but more importantly, you need to know how to overcome the flaws in the basic design of the human mind. We are lacking the natural gift of entry into the unconscious mind. We have to learn how to develop that capability, and this book is designed to give you that skill—and more.

THE WORKBOOK FORMAT

The fourth wheel of our chariot is built around the way this book will take you through your journey. The design is that of a workbook with *living exercises*. We'll use made up dreams and stories such as the kind you or anyone else may have had or might have. And we'll work with your own dreams and stories as well.

This is a hands on book. In fact, working over live exercises is just about the only way you can really appreciate the depth and scope of your dreams and harness their creative powers for your own benefit. We will keep at it, repeating lessons and concepts and methods, and working with dreams and stories until it all becomes familiar and you become an expert dream decoder.

Chapter 2

Introducing Dreams

This chapter will introduce you to dreams and walk you through some of their more elusive but important properties and functions. To understand dream decoding, it is helpful to know that:

1. The *surface* of a dream or the *manifest dream*, as it's called, has a measure of meaning, but these meanings tend to be superficial, self-evident, and of little consequence in our emotional lives.
2. The surface dream as dreamt tells a direct story, but at the same time, it also tells an *indirect* or *encoded (disguised)* story.
3. The encoded story in dreams addresses the most powerful issues of our emotional lives. Dreams report our *unconscious* efforts to cope with and adapt to emotionally charged events. These *trigger experiences* hold the key to decoding our dreams because the disguised meanings of the images and themes in a dream are shaped by these trigger events.
4. Trigger decoding is therefore the means by which we extract a dream's most compelling and disguised meanings.
5. The associations to the elements of a dream— so-called *guided associations*—are an essential part of the dream network. They add an enor-

mous amount of power and meaning to the processing and understanding of a dream.

No dream can be truly and deeply fathomed without strong guided associations to its elements.

6. The thinking and processing behind a dream image is very different from our conscious thinking and processing efforts. Conscious thinking takes one thought at a time and allows but one, directly expressed meaning to each thought we have. On the other hand, unconscious thinking creates images that represent or stand for themselves and several other things all at once.

- *Each single image is a condensation or representation of multiple people, places, and events.*
- *Unconscious thinking also is never directly stated; it is always conveyed via displaced, disguised or encoded images.*
- *Condensation and disguise are ever-present in unconsciously fashioned images.*

7. In looking at a dream, you can ask: what are its evident and directly stated meanings? But you can also ask: What else do these images mean? What are their triggers? What reaction to what event does this dream disguise?

Dreams are stories, and stories are unusual communications that are produced simultaneously by two different parts of our minds: the conscious system and the deep unconscious system. Remarkably, then, the same story has been forged in keeping with two different sets of rules of thinking and gives off two distinctive messages on that basis. You pay your money and you make your choice of the level of meaning you want to invest in.

In this book, we're mainly going to commit ourselves to encoded meanings because they happen to be where the action is.

With this in mind, let's get down to cases. We'll begin with a dream.

EXERCISE

Anne, a young woman in her twenties, dreams she is watching a parade. A man sneaks up on her from behind, spins her around and gives her a kiss. She lingers with the kiss until she realizes that he has a knife in his hand. She pulls back and screams, but he disappears into the crowd, his blonde hair waving in the wind.

QUESTION 2.1

What's in a dream? What can we say on looking at the surface of a dream? What do we learn about Anne? About dreams? About the human mind? Whatever answers occur to you, write them down in the space provided below.

ANSWER 2.1

First off, it's well to notice that this dream is a story. If Anne were telling it to us, we'd say she was narrating her dream. By and large, dreams tend to take a *narrative* form. And narratives, as we will see, are the carriers of both direct and encoded messages or meanings. Our goal is to discover what narratives, such as dreams, tell us about ourselves and others, and about our emotional concerns—and especially their solutions.

Looking directly at this dream it would seem that it's not easy to glean much of importance from the surface of the dream. Whatever impressions we might develop would be surrounded by an air of uncertainty. Yet all is not lost.

The surface contents of a dream often reflect a dreamer's more superficial emotional concerns and issues.

It may be difficult to get a clear sense of the messages being conveyed in a manifest dream, but dream stories as such do tell us something about the dreamer and the people and issues in his or her life.

Then what does this dream tell us about Anne?

In answering this kind of question, it's always best to first state the strongest possible answer, and, from there, go on to less compelling responses. *Power* is always at issue in the world of unconscious experience.

In this case, the strongest statement we can make is that it appears that Anne has a view of men as impulsive, selfish, seductive, dangerous, and running away from her. We could also speculate that Anne may be experiencing conflicts in her relationships with men. Notice the man sneaking up on Anne, his stealing a kiss and holding a knife, Anne's cry of alarm, and his disappearance. This certainly is not a positive picture of a kiss or of a man. Men seem to be dangerous in Anne's mind.

THE SURFACE OF A DREAM

In order to fathom the surface of a dream, proceed cautiously to summarize its main images and their implications.

Surface dreams occur when the dreamer is asleep and the mind is arranged differently from when we're awake.

As a result, concerns and issues that were not sharply in focus when we're awake may come into bold relief when we're asleep and dreaming. The surface of a dream is a fresh take on the emotional world and issues of a dreamer. Some issues are familiar; others may be unexpected. The surface of a dream therefore can serve as a guide to identifying a dreamer's superficial, emotional issues, his or her ways of coping and the like.

We will explore the surface dream more carefully in Chapter 7. For the moment, we simply want to get acquainted with what the surface of a dream has to offer and also what it can never tell us.

> *Looking at a surface dream in isolation makes it all but impossible to tell if you're dealing with a dreamer's response to real issues in his or her life, or with the dreamer's own imagination and fantasies.*

Without knowing more about Anne and her present life circumstances, we're faced with a critical problem: there's no guaranteed way to decide what is real and what is imagined in these dream images. People who work with only the surface of dreams do not realize how crucial this problem is. They take the dream as a product of the mind and imagination of the dreamer and only vaguely, if at all, connect the dream to the real events in his or her life.

But it's very important to know if Anne's dream reveals her own problems in relating to men, or if the dream reflects an actual hurtful and traumatic experience that Anne has suffered at the hands of a man. Is it mainly in Anne's mind that men are dangerous or has a man hurt Anne in some way so that her view of men is deservedly jaundiced? Reality counts a lot in this life of ours, and the isolated surface of a dream makes it difficult to know the shape that it has taken.

After all, we want to use dreams to understand ourselves and those around us. We'd like to be able to draw out solutions to our emotionally charged problems, and develop coping strategies that will improve how we're dealing with these issues directly and consciously. But to do that we need to know the actual problem the dream is dealing with or adapting to. It is essential, then, to know exactly what sets dreams off, what they are a response to, or the nature of their *evocative triggers.*

Anne would search for one kind of solution if she were plagued by inner anxieties and destructive fantasies and memories related to men. She would engage in a rather different pursuit if she were dealing with the real world in the form of some recent hurt. In one case, she would mainly need to heal her inner mind, but in the other case, she'd need to find ways of becoming involved with better male partners (and to heal her mind so she didn't need and find hurtful ones).

In all, the surface of a dream is like a bunch of scattered clues to a mystery. From this it follows that:

> *The greatest value in dreams lies not with their surface meanings, but with their underlying encoded messages.*

The surface dream gives us something, but what it gives us is too confusing, uncertain, and incomplete to be of much use. Surface impressions are more of a first foray and starting point for processing a dream than they are a solution and a deeply insightful end point.

DREAMS AND COPING

> *Dreams are coping or adaptive responses to the emotionally charged events of the dream day.*

To understand the deepest and most important meanings of a dream, you must know the nature of the real events to which the dream is a response. Back now to a key point: dreams need to be framed, to be worked over in context. To fathom the depths of a dream, we need to know the real events with which the dream is an effort to cope.

Suppose you had a picture of Anne with her hands protecting her face. You'd want to know the surrounding realities. Is she protecting herself from attack? Or is she hiding her face because she is embarrassed by something she or someone else said? Or is she soothing a wound that had been inflicted a moment ago, or touching her face in joy and ecstasy on seeing her lover approach?

The meaning of an act is defined by its stimulus, the *trigger* to which it is a response. In the same way, a dream's meaning lies with its stimulus or trigger. A dream is an adaptive response and can be understood only in light of the trigger event to which it is a reaction.

Knowing the nature of a surface act is empty knowledge. To know that Anne is covering her face states a trivial and obvious piece of information, just as knowing that she dreamt of a seductive and assaultive man is trivial and obvious. You've got to know the trigger to know the deeper meaning of the images.

The analogy breaks down at this point because with dreams, you must also know how to undo their disguises. Dreams differ from actions, which are directly observable, in that the main function of dreams is to encode or disguise a response rather than directly state it.

> Whatever direct stimulus you can link up to a dream, there is a hidden and indirect stimulus or trigger lurking about to which the encoded meanings of the dream are a coping response.

Surface dreams are like that picture of Anne. They tell you something but it's quite incomplete and trivial. We sense that Anne appears to have a problem with men. Instead of settling for that pronouncement and keeping it in a vacuum, let's ask, where does the problem come from, what's happened to set off these concerns at the present moment? What has triggered her troubled dream about the blonde man?

QUESTION 2.2

Can you think of a real event or trigger that could have set off Anne's dream? In answering, make use of the themes in her dream.

> *Dream themes are clues to triggers because the themes embrace meaningful reactions to the triggering event to which they are a response.*

What could have prompted Anne to have this particular dream? Try to come up with at least two possibilities. Think of the dream as a mirror of reality and of dream themes as extractions of trigger events. Themes and triggers are like antigens and antibodies, they fit together. The themes in Anne's dream are clues to her trigger experience.

Among the many possible answers to this question, Anne could have been accosted in the street by a man who stole her purse, or hit her, or tried to harm her in some way.

As you can see, dream themes are *translations* of trigger events—dreams of assault are triggered by physical or psychological assaults, while dreams of abandonment reflect experiences of loss of some kind, emotionally or in reality.

To state the main points:

- *Dreams come to life and make serious sense only when their triggers—the real events to which they are a response—are known.*
- *As reflections of unconscious coping efforts, dreams must be deciphered or decoded in light of their triggers.*
- *Every dream is a response to several strong triggers.*
- *The themes of a dream are reactions to, and therefore clues to, the triggers for the dream.*

DREAMS ARE TRIGGERED BY EMOTIONALLY CHARGED EVENTS

Upon asking Anne what could have triggered this dream, what had happened to her on the day of the dream that had some emotional power, she tells us that just two days before her dream she had gotten engaged to Eric, who, in her eyes, is a blonde god. Oddly enough, she muses, both her father and her boss at work (she is the head of personnel for a large corporation) also have blonde hair, as did a man who had tried to mug her by grabbing at her purse on the day of the dream.

Anne has actually given us two triggers for her dream. Can you identify them?

The first trigger is Anne's engagement to Eric, while the second is the stranger's attempt to mug her.

QUESTION 2.4

When a dream is a response to a trigger, there are themes that bridge over from the dream to the trigger event, otherwise known as *bridging themes*. These should be identified first before further processing a dream; they are the means by which we establish the connection between the trigger event and the dream imagery.

For each of these triggers for Anne's dream, identify one or more bridging themes.

ANSWER 2.4

The engagement to Eric is represented by the man who kisses Anne and his blonde hair. The mugger is represented by the man holding a knife in his hand and his having blonde hair as well.

Notice that most of the themes of the dream fit rather well with the attempted mugging. On the other hand, it's not immediately apparent why getting engaged to Eric would evoke a dream of assault and flight. We need to know more about Anne and her triggers to explain that mystery. It may well be that she is anxious about the engagement or that unconsciously she has picked up something hurtful about Eric. It is also possible that there may be yet another powerful trigger to which this dream is a response. There is considerable intrigue to pursuing the deeper meanings of dreams.

QUESTION 2.5

This single dream is the response to how many triggers? Similarly, how many men does the blonde man stand for? Can you see something unique about the dream's images? Do they simply stand for themselves or do they represent many things at once?

ANSWER 2.5

This single dream is a communication about at least two triggers: Anne's engagement and the attempted mugging.

This means that the same dream simultaneously can convey images and meanings that are responsive to two or more triggers.

In thinking things through *consciously*, we are constrained to work over one problem at a time. This is not the case with thinking done outside of awareness. *Unconscious thinking* or *processing* deals with several issues at the same time. The dream report on this processing combines the dreamer's adaptive reactions to several emotionally charged problems into a series of discrete images, each of which portrays specific responses to the various trigger events that have occupied the dreamer unconsciously.

Notice the following:

1. Each individual dream image *combines* or *condenses* a dreamer's unconscious perceptions of several different trigger events.

2. This way of thinking and processing information and meaning is called *thinking via condensation*.

3. Through condensation, the unconscious mind can process and cope with multiple stimuli or triggers via single thoughts or images, which means that every dream image or dream element is the product of condensation. *Each element therefore represents several different events or individuals.*

4. As we will see, as the dreamer *associates* to his or her dream, the specific people and events condensed into each single dream image are revealed.

5. Conscious thinking and coping is carried out in sequence with single meanings, one by one, while unconscious thinking and coping is done with condensed, multiple meaning images, and several at a time. This is one of the most distinctive features of unconscious processing

and of the dreams it generates. And it gives unconscious adaptation a great advantage over conscious adaptation in the emotional realm.

QUESTION 2.6

Condensation was evident in another way in Anne's dream. Did you notice how it was revealed?

ANSWER 2.6

The image of the blonde man in Anne's dream appears to represent or stand for at least four different men in Anne's life: Eric, the mugger, Anne's father, and her boss. Each of these men had blonde hair and therefore could easily be portrayed through a single image of a stranger with blonde hair. Condensed images cleverly take advantage of shared traits to represent multiple people or events. For example, a dream of an accident could represent several different accidents, each of a different kind, or a dream of a thin woman could represent several different women and even a few men as well.

If Anne were to associate to each of these blonde men, we would find that there are one or more stories connected with each of them. It is fair to say that the simple image of a man with blonde hair is a marker for a multitude of narrative themes, which are condensed into a single dream picture. Each of these stories carries several encoded messages in response to trigger events. The accumulation of meaning around a single image is enormous. You can see how condensation gives unconscious thinking tremendous advantages over the more discrete, linear, single-meaning way we think things out consciously.

We need to highlight some additional points.

6. Through condensation and multiple representation, each element of a dream has packed into it and stands for a series of elaborate stories. And each of these stories reflects the underlying meanings of a dream—the issues with which the dream deals and the solutions that are encoded into the dream as well.

7. The key point for the moment is that the surface dream stands for far more than meets the eye directly; the surface dream is like the proverbial tip of an iceberg.

8. If you confine yourself to working with the surface dream, you loose an enormous amount of information and meaning, including the most important aspects of dream communication. Thus, the power of the dream lies in what is disguised and represented, rather than in direct imagery and statements.

9. The substance of dreams is revealed by associating to a dream, especially when those associations are storied in form.

Anne's associations to her dream provided us with an enormous amount of meaning that is unavailable in the surface dream per se. One of the most important maxims for processing dreams states that:

> *Dreams are dreamt to be associated to and processed, rather than analyzed directly.*

DREAM DISGUISE OR ENCODING

Another distinctive feature of dream thinking and representation is the use of disguise or encoding. I already have indicated that a surface dream image stands for itself and many other situations and people. This means that a surface dream image can disguise or encode a variety of people, events, and meanings. We saw that the blonde man represented or encoded four different blonde men. Quite often, however, the mind uses more complex disguises than this. As you might expect, the use of disguise is revealed through associating to a dream.

> *Associating to dreams is one key to their processing and to the revelation of their deepest meanings; the other key is the trigger events.*

Consider now Anne's associations to the dream element of the man running off. The image was associated to an incident from Anne's childhood in which she witnessed her parents quarreling in the street over what she later understood to be her father's involvement with another woman. The argument ended with her mother running off and leaving Anne and her father behind. Soon after the quarrel, Anne's father left her mother and Anne and her brother to live with the other woman, although he later returned and reconstituted his marriage to Anne's mother.

QUESTION 2.7

These associations to the single element of the man's flight in Anne's dream reflect the operation of both condensation and disguise or encoding. What has been condensed into this surface dream image of the man running off? And how does that dream element disguise, encode, or represent something other than its manifest contents of a strange blonde man running away?

ANSWER 2.7

The dream element of the man's flight condenses both Anne's mother running off (men can indeed represent women and *vice versa*) and her father leaving the family. Neither of these incidents are evident on the surface of Anne's dream, yet both are rich in meaning. It seems evident that even though Anne had not thought about these incidents consciously in a long time, her unconscious processing of her engagement had led her to bring forth these memories as part of her working through the implications of her pending marriage to Eric.

> *Dream thinking and the processing it reflects has access to memories that are unavailable to awareness.*

This is another way in which the unconscious processing of an emotional issue is superior to conscious processing. And given that unconscious processing is barely, if at all, reflected in a dream as dreamt (the surface dream), we see again the limitations of work with the surface of a dream. This speaks too for the need for associations to dream elements so the imagery and themes in a dream network can be widened and enriched, thereby revealing the deeper processing of trigger events.

Notice another major point: the condensed images and themes in a dream are always a reaction to contemporaneous, currently active trigger events. The past is awakened in response to issues in the present and as part of our working over and coping with those issues. In processing a dream, it is essential always to find an immediate trigger event to account for the dream imagery.

As for the use of disguise, the blonde stranger's flight encodes the flights of both Anne's mother and her father. The street where Anne is kissed in her dream encodes the street on which her parents argued, and Anne's kiss from a stranger with a knife may well encode her father's affair with another woman.

Incidentally, these associations and encoded memories shed light on why Anne would have an anxious dream upon becoming engaged to Eric. The prospect of marriage is linked in her mind with betrayal, infidelity, and loss; expectations condensed and encoded into her surface dream.

We can now highlight some further points:

1. Dream communication in its most vital form is never straightforward. *Dreams always say one thing and mean something else.* Condensation and encoding are inherent to the thinking behind dream images. Thus dreams always disguise the unconscious mind's responses to hidden or repressed aspects of trigger events.

2. In decoding a dream, these encoding processes must be reversed: the effects of both condensation and disguise must be undone. The encoded image must be decoded to reveal the raw perception behind the dream image. This is done by discovering the hidden trigger for the dream imagery and linking the themes of the dream to the trigger event; connected to their triggers, the themes embody the secret messages of the dream image.

3. Whenever you hear about someone's dream or look at your own dream, your mind set should be: what do these images represent or encode; what else can these images stand for; where is the active trigger for these themes; and what can developing *guided associating* to the dream elements add to the pool of themes and

to our understanding of the dreamer's reactions to the prevailing trigger events?

4. In the world of conscious experience, you take a communication at face value; in the world of unconscious experience, you take nothing at face value—you think of stories as being disguised communications and you always seek to undo that disguise in light of the prevailing, active triggers.

5. The images in a surface dream reflect the surface people, places, and events of the dream, but, in addition, these same images also encode or disguise one or more additional people, places, and events.

6. The contents and meanings that are disguised in a dream are far more critical than those that appear on the surface of the dream—this, too, is another major limitation of working with a surface dream by itself.

DREAMS AND SECRET PROBLEMS—AND THEIR SOLUTIONS

We've seen that dreams are triggered by emotionally important events and that they reflect our unconscious efforts to cope with these events. Anne's dream could be worked over to reveal reactions to her engagement, to the attempted mugging, to a recent incident with her father, and to another incident with her boss. In each case, Anne was hurt in some way that she had not realized until she had decoded her dream. And in each case, she saw that she was warning herself to be wary of these men and protect herself from harm. "Stop being attracted to dangerous men," was Anne's warning to herself through the image of her lingering with the kiss until she realized that the man had a knife and withdrew. While Anne had not thought this way consciously in each of the situations with the men she knew (her fiance, father, and boss), she did think that way unconsciously.

Let's close out this introduction to dreams with a particular association Anne had to her dream. As you will see, I selected this association to show you that dreams embody reactions to problems that are not at all apparent in the surface dream and not within the general awareness of the dreamer. That is, we suffer through many emotional traumas quite unaware consciously of our hurts and their nature. Yet all the while, these hurts register unconsciously or subliminally and are worked over outside of awareness and revealed in encoded form through our dreams.

Each element of a dream is exquisitely fashioned by the unconscious mind to communicate a multiplicity of messages and meanings. The parade in Anne's dream, for example, led her to remember a parade she had seen as a child with her father and from there she went to a Fourth of July picnic she had gone to with Eric and then to a commercial show she had gone to with her boss. Each of these associated stories brought forth images and themes relevant to one of the main triggers that had set off Anne's dream in the first place: her engagement to Eric.

But then quite unexpectedly Anne remembered a parade she had gone to with her Uncle Fred, her mother's brother. Anne was about eleven at the time and he had been quite physical with her, touching her again and again. From then on, Anne made it a point never to be alone with him. Later, Anne found out that Fred, who was married, had had an affair with a woman at work.

This led Anne to another related association. It involved Mark, a man at work, who had been developing a project with Anne during the past three months. Now that she thought about him, Anne realized that Mark liked to put his hand on her arm when he talked with her. Anne had some sense that Mark—who was not married—was an attractive man, but she had not consciously entertained fantasies of being involved with him.

With her associations directing her to Mark, Anne suddenly remembered that on the day of her dream she had met with Mark to discuss their joint project. As they talked, Mark had begun to play with a letter opener that looked a lot like a knife. While he was doing it, he told Anne about his recent break-up with his girlfriend. Without thinking, Anne had suggested that they get back to work and have a drink after hours so they could talk. She had felt a bit uncomfortable later on when they did have that drink and Mark had revealed his soul to her. And to her surprise, now that she thought about it, Mark also has blonde hair.

QUESTION 2.8

Have these associations unearthed a hidden trigger for Anne's dream? If so, what is it and what are the images that bridge from the associations to the trigger event?

ANSWER 2.8

These associations do indeed reveal a repressed or obliterated and forgotten set of interrelated triggers for Anne's dream. The triggers are Mark's touching Anne, his revelations to her about his personal life, and his having a drink with her at a bar. The *bridging imagery* includes the letter opener that looked like a knife and Mark's blonde hair—a manifest element that apparently encoded and represented not four, but at least five different men!

QUESTION 2.9

Anne's conscious reaction to these triggers was to have the drink with Mark and hear him out. She was not aware of much beyond that. What however does the dream and Anne's associations to it reveal about her unconscious experience and perceptions of these triggers from Mark?

ANSWER 2.9

In her dream, Anne encodes Mark as an intrusive man who kisses her and has a dangerous weapon—a knife. In the dream Anne lingers with the kiss and this encodes her unconscious attraction to Mark. Outside of direct awareness, she also had perceived his attraction to her and this, too, is represented in the kiss. And given Anne's associations to her father's and uncle's affairs, we can see that Anne was struggling with thoughts of betraying Eric by having an affair with Mark.

QUESTION 2.10

Anne's dream and her associations suggest how she should handle her hidden attraction. What is that suggestion?

ANSWER 2.10

In her surface dream Anne pulls away from the blonde man, frightened by the knife he is carrying. In this way, her deep unconscious system was telling her to not get involved with Mark (was there a warning about her engagement condensed into this image as well?).

But perhaps the most sage, adaptive solution is offered in Anne's association to her Uncle Fred. The theme that bridges from Fred to Mark is that of touching—physical contact. And in her recollection of her uncle's inappropriate seductiveness (much as Mark's seductiveness also was inappropriate in light of Anne's engagement), Anne recalls her decision to never be alone with him again.

Stay away from inappropriately seductive men—such is the sensible advice Anne's deeply unconscious wisdom system offered to her. Were she to decode her dream and her associations, her way of handling Mark would be quite clear to her. Without trigger decoding the dream, Anne is likely to waffle in her feelings toward her coworker—the conscious mind tends to be quite uncertain about most emotionally charged issues.

We can see then that:

1. Dreams and the unconscious perceptions and processing that they convey are in touch with emotional issues that elude awareness.
2. Processing a dream by associating to its elements and allowing the emergent themes to point to missing triggers enables you to discover and work with the other half of your emotional life—the important part that flows along outside of awareness.
3. Dreams deal with *hidden* triggers that emotionally are remarkably strong and they offer fine solutions to the issues raised by these unconsciously traumatic events.

SUMMING UP

The surface of a dream is similar to the camouflage used to hide secret weapons and other evidence of danger and criminality. You can spend your time studying the false front provided by the disguise, but, as you can see, you'll not be at the level where things get serious and important. You may learn a thing or two, but what you learn really isn't that surprising or meaningful in the scheme of things. The power of the situation is underneath the camouflage, disguised in the surface deception. And to get at that deeper power, you need both the triggers and the associations connected with your dream. How you do this will, of course, be developed as this book unfolds.

To summarize, here are some of the points developed in this chapter:

1. Working with surface dreams by themselves is a trivial pursuit.
2. Dreams (and stories) are remarkable communications that embody both direct and disguised or encoded meanings. The latter are where the action of your emotional life is worked over and affected.
3. There are two ways of approaching a dream. The first is in terms of its manifest images and the conscious issues that they reflect. The second is to consider the dream as an encoded or disguised message that has a multiplicity of meanings condensed into each of its elements; this view implies that dreams need to be decoded in light of the trigger events to which they are responsive. In the first way of thinking, an image is what it is and no more, but in the second way of thinking, an image is a disguised message that needs unmasking.
4. The power of our emotional lives is not available in the manifest dream-conscious experience realm, but it is available in the encoded content-unconscious experience realm.

5. Decoding dream images and their themes in light of their evocative triggers is the only known means through which we can enter, master and use the wisdom of the deep intelligence that is brought to bear on our unconscious emotional experiences.

If you've lost interest in much of the surface dream and have acquired an interest the capacity of images and language to communicate encoded messages, then you are ready to move on. Before we do so, let's close out this chapter by turning one of your own dreams.

EXERCISE

Remember your most recent dream. If you can't think of a current dream, make up a very short story with a beginning, middle, and end and then use it as your dream for this exercise. Once you've thought of the dream, think about the people and the setting, action, and themes of the dream.

QUESTION 2.11

What are the main themes in your dream? Try to list the strongest themes first followed by the weaker ones.

ANSWER 2.11

Listing dream themes should give you a sense of the power of your dream and the issues that it is trying to deal with.

Themes are the clues to triggers—themes and triggers complete the circle you need for trigger decoding your dreams.

Try next to think of your main experiences on the day of the dream. Search for emotionally important moments, such as major traumas and successes and less compelling incidents. As a framework for these efforts, recognize that, as is true of all organs of the human body, the human mind is designed to cope with environmental inputs: incidents, interactions with others, and the like.

The human mind is an organ of adaptation, which is why dreams must be deciphered in light of their evocative triggers.

QUESTION 2.12

Think about the themes of your dream. Do they bridge over and connect to the trigger events you've already identified? Do they also suggest triggers you haven't listed?

ANSWER 2.12

If you've identified an emotionally important trigger, the themes of your dream should shed light on how you unconsciously experienced the trigger event. Once your trigger list is in place, look over your dream and try to see what the dream is communicating about those triggers. Themes that do not seem to connect to the triggers you've already identified suggest that one or more significant triggers are repressed or missing. Try to allow your unexplained themes to point you toward these missing triggers.

We'll sharpen up this skill as we go along, so try here to simply get a sense of how the dream images and themes connect to the triggers you've identified.

Finally, associate to one or two of your dream elements. Make sure these so-called guided associations are in the form of some kind of story. Most often they will pertain to an incident in your own life.

Once these fresh stories are finished, look over their themes. List the main themes and select those that are most powerful. Compare the themes in the manifest dream with the themes in your associations to the dream. As a rule, the associated themes will be stronger than the themes in the surface dream. But in addition, these fresh themes often will point to unrecognized triggers—emotionally charged events you hadn't realized you were reacting to. Try to use your themes to discover at least one trigger you hadn't realized was an issue for you.

All this has been in the way of giving you a chance to work over or play with your dreams, to feel them out, to sense the richness of what they convey, and to get a line on how to process your dream so you can unearth encoded, unconscious meanings. This exercise has hopefully given you a feeling for dreams and the associations to dreams, and for triggers and themes. The intention is to open new avenues for processing dreams and to make you aware of how much lies beyond the surface of a dream.

With that accomplished, we'll soon go through the processing of a dream step by step. However, before that, let's introduce the "cousins" of dreams—stories or narratives. They, too, are magnificent carriers of both conscious and unconscious meaning and they are far more ubiquitous than most people realize.

Chapter 3

Story Lines
and Narratives

We have seen that dreams are, by and large, storied tales. I have argued that dreams draw their inordinate power from their storied lines which is the most fundamental property of emotionally charged communication. Yet the understanding of unconscious experience and unconscious communication has centered on dreams rather than stories.

We can readily appreciate how this came about. It's far easier to isolate a dream than it is to isolate and process a story. Most stories are told in the course of conversations in which the mind is set for conscious issues and attention to surface contents; they are part of the conscious world of experience. As a result, we fail to appreciate the powerful encoded messages they also contain. For that, we need to invoke a different way of thinking. And of course, Sigmund Freud, the man who is credited for getting so much of our understanding of unconscious processing started, used dreams as his foil, and others have followed suit.

We've mistakenly come to think of dreams—as Freud put it—as the royal road to the unconscious. The truth is that narratives, stories of any kind, are the royal road and dreams are one type of narrative among many. Novels, myths, fairy tales, folk tales, newspaper stories, movies, plays, fantasies, day dreams, and similar storied communications have been with us since the origins of language and possibly even earlier through bodily communication and mime. And scientific research has shown that when we communicate with others, we consistently rotate in and out of storied expressions; telling tales one moment and analyzing and intellectualizing the next, only to return to story telling soon again. This rotation is a fundamental property of human communication.

The present chapter will introduce storied lines. These are the main points that will be developed:

1. Every story embodies both a conscious and an unconscious message.
2. The stories you make up and those that occur to you in the course of a conversation—*marginally related or coincidental stories*—contain important encoded, unconscious perceptions of the relationship and interaction with the person to whom you tell your tale. Much the same applies to coincidental stories other people tell you; they contain disguised responses to the hidden, unconscious issues that exist between you and them.
3. The keys to decoding marginally related stories lies first, with realizing an encoded message has been emitted and shifting into the decoding mode of thinking (you've got to catch the encoded message to decode it), and second, realizing that the most important trigger for these stories lies in the immediate situation between the story teller and his or her audience.

THE MADE-UP STORY

Stories and dreams essentially are structured in similar fashion. Both forms of expression carry surface (manifest) messages and encoded (latent) messages as well. In practice, stories are in many ways more versatile and serviceable than dreams.

There are two ways that you can make use of the stories that you and others compose. The first is personal and involves creating your own story when you don't have a dream to process; once composed, you simply treat the story as if it were a dream and associate to its elements and find its triggers. A great deal of dream processing is done at night before going to sleep or while engaged in solitary activities that are not overly demanding on one's attention, such as driving a car, riding a train, or taking a break from work. If you want to process a dream and can't find one to process, the made-up story will serve you well.

The made-up story is every bit as serviceable as a dream, which means you are always in a position to process a dream equivalent when you want to get in touch with your emotional issues and your own responsive unconscious wisdom. We'll do some exercises with your own made-up stories later in the book (see Chapter 11).

TALES TOLD BY OTHERS

The second use of everyday narratives is extremely useful and of great value in negotiating relationships, business situations, and everything else that has an emotional charge to it. The belief that dreams and stories are products of the inventive human imagination with only minimal or no relevance to reality is a false myth. The fact is that narratives actually reflect the workings of an unconscious mind that is continuously monitoring our moment-to-moment experiences and is exquisitely in touch with and responsive to these realities, far more so than are our conscious minds which tend to be highly defensive and obliterating its perceptions of emotionally charged trigger events.

In every emotionally important situation with one or more persons, every story that you think of (and should keep to yourself) and every story another person tells you contains not only a set of conscious meanings, but also a set of unconscious meanings. Remarkably, the unconscious meanings always pertain to the immediate situation itself. That is, these coincidentally recalled or marginally related stories always encode the unconscious experience of the narrator as it pertains to the interaction within which it is told.

You are talking to your boss about a business problem and he tells you a story about someone in another company or about something that happened to him or her today, yesterday, or whenever. You're talking to your significant other about a problem that has cropped up and you think of something you read in the newspaper or he or she tells you about a movie they've seen.

These are examples of *coincidental* or *marginally related* stories that come to mind in the course of a conversation or dialogue. Their main attribute is that they are not part of the direct discussion or negotiations at hand, but are brought up as an aside.

The key to processing a marginally related story is shifting into the decoding mode of thinking, without which you are certain to take the story at face value and miss its encoded messages.

Making good use of marginally related stories lies in recognizing that a coincidental story has just been told and that it has two levels of meaning. Again, the first level is on the surface and lies in the tale as it is told. But the second and more emotionally crucial level of meaning is disguised or encoded in that same surface tale. And as I said, the main trigger for the encoded messages always lies within the situation and relationship at hand.

If you're talking to someone and they offer an aside story, they're revealing in disguised fashion how they are unconsciously perceiving what you are doing and saying. If you yourself think of a marginally related story, then you are encoding your own unconscious impressions of the other person and marking out the unconscious issues between you and them. When involved in a going-nowhere, circular argument with someone, only a coincidental story will tell you what the far stronger unconscious issue is all about—the deeper reasons why nothing is getting resolved.

There's a great advantage to processing stories rather than dreams. Dreams are dreamt at the end of a day in response to a myriad of trigger events. Each dream therefore works over, through condensation and disguise, many triggers at once, diluting its concentration on a single trigger event. The same description applies to a story you make up for processing in the absence of a recent dream.

On the other hand, a story thought of or told while interacting with another person or persons reflects the unconscious working over of one overriding trigger event—the present interaction between yourself and them. With the trigger known, the themes can be used to reveal the unconscious problems currently at hand and their best resolution. The information you derive from this effort is invaluable; you are tapping into unconscious experiences that have enormous power when it comes to the outcome of a conversation, interaction, and relationship. And besides, a properly decoded, made-up story puts you in possession of insights that only the unconscious mind has access to, and highly valuable insights at that. It gives you information and understanding that neither you nor the other person have consciously, information that can save a relationship or a situation.

EXERCISE

John is an attorney. He is sitting with Judy who is in the process of getting divorced. She is interviewing John so she can decide if he should be her lawyer in this matter.

John advocates a strong approach to the divorce and he stresses how crucial it is that Judy get every penny due her, and then some, even if it takes some twisting of the truth to do it. He goes on and on about how he has ways of dealing with tough guys like Judy's husband and his attorney.

After listening for a while, Judy speaks up. "I certainly want everything I'm entitled to," she begins, "but I'm not sure I have the stomach for a fight. I don't know how I feel about it."

John argues that she shouldn't be a masochist and let herself be exploited. Again, he presses his point: you've got to fight fire with fire.

Judy agrees she should get what she's entitled to. And John may be right about how to do go about getting it, but she's not sure he is. But then again, she certainly doesn't want to let her husband walk all over her.

Judy then says, "You know, divorces are difficult and so is what happens after a divorce. I guess you know all about that. I saw this story in a magazine. It seems this woman had divorced her husband so she could live with another man who she'd been having an extra-marital affair with. The husband was so agitated by what had gone on that he insisted on seeing his ex-wife to talk things out again. When they met, they began to quarrel and he lost control, grabbed a knife from the kitchen table and seriously wounded his ex."

"And you know what?" Judy went on, "The man was ready to confess that he had lost it and accept his punishment, when his family hired a shrewd attorney who had him plead temporary insanity and got him acquitted of attempted murder. The ex-wife had written the article to complain about the justice system and comment on belligerent divorces and manipulative attorneys. What a mess," Judy concluded, "just reading about it gave me a headache for two days. How can people be like that with each other—it's not human. And that attorney, he was something else. I guess he was just doing his job, but I'd rather own up to what I did than lie and cheat. That woman never should have let her ex in the door. She would have been far better off if she had steered clear of the likes of him."

QUESTION 3.1

Let's begin our study of coincedental, narrative stories by asking a basic question: is there a narrative tale in this vignette? If so, who tells it and what is it about?

ANSWER 3.1

There is one major coincidental narrative in this material: the magazine story that Judy recounts to John. As I said, you can think of that story as the equivalent of a dream, as a *waking dream,* if you will. It has the same structure as a dream. The main difference is that a dream is dreamt when we are asleep and not attempting to cope with an immediate relationship or problem, while most stories are told in the course of an interaction in which both direct (conscious) and indirect (encoded and unconscious) processing are actively being carried out. A daydream or fantasy is intermediate between a night dream and a story told directly to another person—it is a waking dream that usually is not directed immediately at another person (although it may occur silently in another's presence).

Judy's story was only marginally related to what was being discussed at the moment. On the other hand, if John had asked what had happened to prompt her request for a divorce, the story Judy would then tell would be a directly related narrative tale and could not be treated as having a critical encoded dimension. It is only when we have the relative freedom to generate a story that this allows the mind to create a tale with two levels of meaning: one conscious, the other unconscious.

Judy's story therefore can be taken as one that has some bearing on her discussion with John and, therefore, some degree of direct and conscious relevance. But the same story also *simultaneously encodes an unconscious perception or experience and message* whose nature or meaning we have yet to determine.

QUESTION 3.2

Go back to the anecdote and identify some examples of *nonstoried or nonnarrative* communication. Contrast storied and nonstoried communications in your mind and try to get as sense of how stories readily carry encoded meaning and nonstories tend not to or may do so in some minimal way because intellectualizations are always about something.

ANSWER 3.2

The remaining exchanges between Judy and John are basically nonnarrative in nature. For example, there is John's explanation of how he handles divorce cases, and there is Judy's wish to have her due but to not get into a battle. These are not tales or story lines, but intellectual explanations. They carry little if any encoded meaning. But notice that John's suggestion that he can manipulate the truth to get

Judy what she deserves does have a minimal storied line in that it anticipates an event in which John would lie to get something for his client. Here the narrative aspect is thin, while in Judy's story of the divorced couple it is strong, detailed, and elaborate.

QUESTION 3.3

There are, then, two basic modes of human communication. What are they?

ANSWER 3.3

The two modes of communicative expression are *narrative* (storied) and *nonnarrative* (nonstoried) in form. Stories and nonstories are the two vehicles through which we express ourselves. Narratives include anything with a story line, while nonnarrative communication has many forms such as explanations, analyses, discussions, intellectualizations, statements of facts, directions or advice, and attributes of things and people.

> *The deep unconscious system whose wisdom we seek to capture always communicates by means of detailed storied lines.*
>
> *In contrast to nonstories, the narrative mode is the means by which we convey double messages— messages with both conscious and unconscious meanings.*

If you're trying to determine if an unconscious message has been communicated, you should first determine if a story has been told. If you find a narrative, you can be assured that you have found a vehicle of encoded expression. Thus, the question of possible unconscious activity in our little vignette comes down to seeing if it contains a story told by either Judy or John or both. As we saw, Judy did tell a coincidental story and therefore she alone engaged in clear, active, unconscious expression in this dialogue. John did so to a far lesser degree.

QUESTION 3.4

What is the main trigger for Judy's encoded message?

ANSWER 3.4

Just as dreams are triggered by emotionally charged events, stories also are prompted by similar kinds of experiences. All forms of narrative serve human emotional adaptation, especially unconscious adaptation.

There are in principle several triggers for this story. Some of them undoubtedly are connected with Judy's relationship with her husband and the reasons for her wish for a divorce. If you were thinking of Judy's story as a *displaced* and *encoded* message, it might have occurred to you that one theme in the story is that of an adulterous wife. You then might have wondered if Judy's story was her encoded way of warning John to not go so fast, that Judy had been unfaithful to her husband, and was in a far more vulnerable position than John realized. If you entertained such an idea, you would have been quite right in your formulation.

> *Our stories reveal far more than we consciously realize.*

For the moment, the most pressing and critical trigger for Judy's story is the situation in which she finds herself at the exact instance that she told her story. Thus, the immediate *trigger event* is John's remarks to Judy and their many implications, not a few of which have been *perceived* and *registered unconsciously* in Judy's mind.

In principle, a coincidental story told by a party to a dialogue, whatever its manifest reasons and contents, always encodes the story teller's unconscious perceptions of the other person's comments and behaviors. The conjured-up story is a dream equivalent manufactured on the spot to reflect the teller's unconscious experience and his or her reactions to that experience. If you want to be in touch with the world of unconscious experience (and well you should), you must keep in mind that in addition to their surface meanings and conscious functions, all of these stories have latent, encoded meanings and unconscious functions; they serve unconscious adaptation.

> The deep unconscious system of the human mind—the unconscious part of the mind that composes dreams and selects stories for recall during personal interactions—is a system that is continuously active and very much locked into the present moment.

While the conscious system (the conscious mind) can range far into the past and future, the unconscious mind stays with the present and touches on the past or future solely in light of the present.

> The deep unconscious system is here-and-now centered.
> It follows then that any story made up or recalled during a given interaction will encode the story-teller's unconscious experience of that interaction.
> The main trigger for a marginally related story is in the present situation and in the words and actions of the other person.

The story reflects the teller's unconscious processing of the other person's inputs into their interaction. It reflects the teller's unconscious perceptions of the other person and, secondarily, of the teller himself or herself, and his or her responses to those perceptions as well.

Dreams and narratives are outer-focused first and inner-focused only secondarily. They are a way of getting in touch with our unconscious experience of the world about us and its impingements on our psyches and then, and only then, with ourselves. This is true of all stories and dreams—they reflect ways of coping. Unconscious experience is as much a part of the flow of our lives as conscious experience; it is active every minute of our lives.

EXERCISE

We'll come back to Judy and John in the next chapter. For now, let's do a personal exercise of your own. Think back over your day, can you remember telling or hearing any marginally related stories? Spend your next day on the alert for these tales, your own and those of others.

QUESTION 3.5

How often do coincidental stories come up? In what kind of situations and relationships? Think of each situation in which a coincidental story was told. Try to get a sense of what evoked the story and what encoded meanings it might have. We'll soon be developing the details of how to trigger decode these tales. For the moment, develop your impressions and see what you can learn from them.

ANSWER 3.5

Coincidental stories are very common. If you haven't detected any or have picked up only one or two in the course of a busy day, you should try again and keep your ears sharply attuned for narrative and storied lines. These stories are especially abundant in emotionally charged situations and relationships. And the longer you're with someone the greater the likelihood he or she will tell one or more coincidental stories.

These stories are communicated to convey one's unconscious experiences. If you tune in on the main themes of such a story, they can be taken to characterize the ways in which the story teller is unconsciously experiencing what is going on with you.

> *Themes are the means by which an encoded story conveys its unconscious messages. Themes bridge from the direct, surface story to the unmentioned trigger event that they characterize.*

Historically, the exploration of the unconscious realm did not begin with the *stimulus,* but with the *response.* And initially these responses in the form of dreams and stories were not understood to be adaptive reactions to trigger events, but were isolated from immediate experience and treated as entities unto themselves. We did homage to that approach by beginning our own investigation of the unconscious realm of experience by looking first at dreams and stories. But from the outset, we tried to keep in mind that these communications are made in response to real impingements. Let's complete this introduction into the world of unconscious communication, processing, and adaptation with a look at trigger events, which is the subject of the next chapter.

Chapter 4

Triggers Point the Way

An essential feature of dreams and stories is that they are adaptive or coping responses to the events of our lives.

Unconscious processing is carried out in the course of all emotionally tinged experiences that are sufficiently disturbing to automatically be *perceived outside of awareness*—unconsciously or subliminally. We call these incidents *triggers or trigger events* because they trigger or activate a response from the deep unconscious system of the mind and mobilize its deep intelligence. We cope with life within and outside of awareness; narratives are our way of telling ourselves and others about our world of unconscious experience.

The basic principles of decoding dreams and stories follows from the understanding that they are in essence *adaptive responses*.

The narratives of dreams and stories embody the encoded or disguised themes that reflect the nature of our unconscious experiences, while their triggers reveal exactly which events these encoded themes define.

Themes are the bridge from the trigger event to the dream or story; dreams and stories are selected for expression solely because of the themes they embody.

Unconsciously, Judy decided to tell John the magazine story because its themes encoded the unconscious experience of his remarks that she was trying to communicate to him. The resourcefulness of the human mind is simply awesome.

In this chapter we'll get acquainted with some of the basic properties of trigger events and see how they activate the deep unconscious system of the mind. We will take advantage of the finding that marginally related stories are always triggered by events in the situation in which the storyteller finds himself or herself. This makes trigger identification relatively easy, although it is important to tease out the exact aspects of the trigger experience to which the storyteller is responding unconsciously.

To highlight the main ideas we will work over:

- Triggers are the real-life, emotionally charged events to which dreams and stories are a response.
- In processing or decoding a dream or story we are essentially processing or decoding its triggers, the life events the dreamer or storyteller is trying to cope with.
- Triggers are the key to decoding dreams and stories; they organize and give decoded meaning to the themes in narrative networks.
- Decoding dreams and stories means unraveling their disguised themes in light of their evocative trigger events.

In the previous chapter, the primary trigger for Judy's story was her unconscious experience of John's presentation of how he would operate as her divorce attorney. The responsive story that Judy told served to express both her conscious and unconscious impressions of that trigger event.

Let's proceed now to trigger decode Judy's story, to unravel and decipher the disguised meanings in her tale in light of the experiences that evoked her communicated narrative.

Trigger decoding essentially involves linking or connecting the trigger event (including its implications or meanings) to the themes in the reported narrative.

The breakdown of how this works is:

- A trigger is an emotionally charged experience.
- This experience has meaning and content.
- A responsive story encodes or disguises and represents those meanings.
- As a result, the themes in the story mirrors and reflects the themes in the trigger event that evoked the story.

A good way to initiate this effort is to get a sense of the main attributes of the trigger event. What, then, are the salient features of John's presentation to Judy, the trigger for Judy's story?

ANSWER 4.1

It seems fair to say that John's approach was rather forceful, blunt, ruthless, and somewhat dishonest. Whatever Judy's conscious impressions of John's pitch, all of these attributes would be detected unconsciously, especially those qualities that Judy automatically did not allow herself to become aware of. They would then be processed outside of awareness and encoded in her story. The evaluation of the *attributes* of a trigger event serves to orient you so you can organize the themes of the responsive narrative around the implications of the stimulus for the thematic response. It is not uncommon, however, for us to consciously overlook important qualities in a trigger event. This means that it is necessary to keep an open mind when looking over such an event and to use the themes in the encoded story as clues to overlooked attributes of known triggers and for completely missed evocative trigger events as well.

Having identified the main features of the trigger John created, let's turn next to Judy's response.

QUESTION 4.2

To begin on the surface level, what was Judy's *conscious* reaction to John's presentation?

ANSWER 4.2

Consciously, Judy was vague and uncertain about how she felt regarding John's attitude and proposal. She didn't want to get into an unnecessary fight with her husband, but she also didn't want to be a patsy. She therefore was unsure about embracing John's approach to her divorce, which she resisted one moment and accepted the next.

In the emotional realm, this kind of uncertainty is typical of the conscious mind. As long as there is any ambiguity in a situation, we tend to waffle back and forth in our response. In contrast, the deep unconscious system is quite incisive and uncompromising in its thinking about the same events and their implications. This reliable sense of certainty is one of the many advantages to dealing with an emotionally charged trigger event with knowledge of your unconscious picture of the situation. Deep unconscious processing is a far superior instrument of adaptation as compared to conscious processing.

Let's turn now to Judy's *unconscious* perceptions of John's presentation.

QUESTION 4.3

We'll begin with *bridging themes* (themes in the story that actually describe aspects of the trigger event showing that the two are connected). Try to identify at least two themes that bridge or connect Judy's story to the trigger situation with John.

ANSWER 4.3

There are at least two striking bridging themes in Judy's story: divorce and attorneys. Both themes lie within the surface story and also apply to the trigger event. A third theme, that of a man and woman sitting down to talk, is a weaker bridging theme in that it, too, is present in both the coincidental story and in the trigger situation; talking was exactly what Judy and John were doing at the moment. There are, then, several convincing themes in the story that describe and therefore link it to the trigger event.

QUESTION 4.4

Next, identify the most important and strongest themes in Judy's story. Extract the themes from the surface story and keep them in mind for later use. *Theme identification is a vital part of the decoding process.*

ANSWER 4.4

To answer, we must name of all of the strong images in the surface story about the divorced couple. The main themes in Judy's story are those of divorce, argument, violent attack, physical injury, wanting to confess, and getting off scot-free with the help of a shrewd and somewhat dishonest attorney.

Recall now that these themes, which are part of Judy's surface tale, also belong to Judy's *unconscious perceptions* of the trigger event.

> *Human encoding and disguise operates by telling a story about one situation in order to encode a story about another situation: the trigger event.*
> *As you listen to the surface tale, you must ask yourself, what other situation or trigger event does this story apply to as well.*

In our exercise, we know that the trigger event is John's presentation. We can therefore say that Judy's unconscious perceptions of the trigger involves experiences of (themes or images of) divorce, argument, attack, harm, shrewdness, and confession.

Themes in hand, the next step in the process is to take these themes and *apply* them to the trigger event. We organize the themes as reflections of the way Judy, based on her own sensitivities (selectively), has experienced what John has said. We do not treat these images and themes as products of Judy's imagination unrelated to John or as her fantasies or daydreams about him. We see these themes as *reflecting a true and valid picture* of the way in which John actually has expressed himself.

QUESTION 4.5

We are ready now to lift these themes from the original narrative and place them into the trigger situation with John. Try to generate a statement, a small narrative tale, that would begin with the trigger event and proceed to characterize Judy's unconscious view of that event as described by her thematic imagery.

ANSWER 4.5

We can read out these themes as indicating that Judy felt that John was doing violence to her, that he's shady and corrupt, and that she sees him as inclined to act rather than to talk about issues. From Judy's perspective the essential read-out would be: I'm experiencing your approach to my divorce as assaultive, hurtful, dishonest, and thoughtless.

QUESTION 4.6

Encoded stories also contain *reactions* to unconscious perceptions. Using the themes in Judy's story, can you identify her main reaction to her unconscious view of John? The theme you are searching for does not describe a likely attribute of what John's has said—(it is not descriptive of the trigger)—so it therefore must be a response to the perceptions we just stated.

ANSWER 4.6

Judy's themes indicate that she does not want to hire or be associated with a quarrelsome and manipulative attorney like John; she can only be hurt badly by such a man. This unconscious decision was revealed when she remarked that the ex-wife should have avoided people like her ex-husband. The theme of divorce also speaks for the same decision—Judy wants to divorce herself from John.

USING DECODED INSIGHTS

Without adding more to this reading of the latent and unconscious messages and meanings in this story, an important practical consideration emerges. At the point in their meeting when Judy tells John her story, he actually is at a critical crossroads in their interaction. If he fails to trigger decode Judy's narrative and misses its unconscious meanings, he will continue on as he has been doing and he will *not* get Judy as a client. Her unconscious experience of his pitch has alienated her and will frighten her away in fear of being harmed by what he would do.

Judy's plans to turn away from John are encoded in her final comment about the woman in her story. While consciously uncertain of whether to hire John, unconsciously Judy was quite clear about not wanting to do so. And unless a self-hurtful need had been activated (and all too often, it is), she would soon translate her unconscious processing into a conscious decision to walk away from this attorney.

On the other hand, matters could be quite different if John were to shift from the *conscious mode* of listening to the *unconscious mode* of listening when Judy told her tale. While hearing and understanding the implications of the actual story, he would also be saying to himself, "this is a story, an encoded message. Judy is telling this story to me, so it must encode her impressions of my presentation to this point. How am I doing? Someone is being attacked, there's a shady attorney—I'm not doing very well, am I? What have I said to deserve these awful images? Oh, that business about going after her husband and shading the facts. I better clean up my act or I'm not going have this woman as a client."

You enter a different world of experience when you shift to the decoding mode of listening—a world of power and influence well beyond conscious realization. Unconscious communication is everywhere; it is a factor in every situation and it is a part of our adaptive armamentarium. Although unseen, unconscious experience is of enormous influence on our decisions and choices, and it expresses itself with a voice and language that is well worth hearing and understanding.

EXERCISE

Hopefully, you now have a sense of what it means to process a dream or story in order to extract the encoded messages and meanings they contain. Let's move toward concluding this chapter by engaging in a final exercise. This time we will use a specific story you heard from someone you had dealings with or made up yourself in the course of an important conversation with another person or two. The key is that someone told a by-the-way or coincidental story.

It's generally easier to begin with someone else's story, but if you can't recall one (even though they are commonplace, they're often not noticed) then think back and see if you can remember thinking of or telling someone else a marginally related story of your own.

If these two efforts fail you, then spend the rest of today and tomorrow ready to shift into the decoding mode, alert to the emergence of a coincidental story. Capture a story of that kind that you or someone else told.

Now, whatever means you used to get hold of a coincidental story, answer the following questions.

QUESTIONS 4.7

Identify the most powerful *themes* in the marginally related story you have in mind.

Next, mark the situation in which that story was thought of or told. What are the main attributes of the situation, of the trigger event to which the story was a response?

Now, attempt to find at least one or two bridging themes that connect the coincidental story to the trigger event.

With the bridging themes in hand, take the power themes in the marginally related story and formulate their main meanings as the storyteller's *unconscious perceptions* of the trigger event. Develop a decoded story that begins with the trigger event and uses the themes to characterize how it was experienced. Use our work with Judy's story as your guide and do the best you can pending the specific exercises in linking that will be offered later in the book.

The marginally related story should encode a perception of the trigger event within which it was told. That is, the themes of the story should address an unconscious issue between the storyteller and the other person. It is important to get used to taking the themes in a story or dream and shaping them as valid unconscious perceptions of the trigger event.

Think of trigger decoding and linking as describing what your eyes unconsciously saw and your ears unconsciously heard.

SUMMING UP

These are the main points to keep in mind about coincidental stories:

1. Everyone rotates in and out of story telling; narrative communication is a fundamental property of human expression.
2. We experience the world on two levels: consciously and unconsciously. Both conscious and unconscious experiences are continuous and both flow as separate but related streams of human life.

3. In every situation and interaction we engage in, there is both conscious and unconscious experience. Quite naturally, we know a great deal about the former and virtually nothing about the latter which is encoded in our stories and unavailable to awareness unless we engage in trigger decoding.

4. In the course of our daily lives and the transactions we have with others—family, friends, business associates, teachers and students—there are two levels of interaction: conscious and unconscious. This second level, unconscious experience, exerts an unseen but powerful effect on the first level, the conscious experience.

5. The ways in which we react to others, the short- and long-term decisions we make each day, our emotional state, and behaviors are silently driven by the nature of our particular unconscious perceptions and experiences. The conscious mind simply makes up rationalizations with which to justify or excuse our unconsciously driven responses in the surface world in which we interact with others. By and large, our unconscious minds are in charge of our emotional lives.

6. In practical terms: in the course of an interaction, no matter what its nature, whenever we think of a story or hear a story from another person, we should shift into the unconscious or decoding mode of listening and thinking. In this mode, if the story is told by the other person, you must realize that the stories contain themes that need to be detached from their surface context and linked to the trigger events

that you have created. The reverse applies to your own stories, their themes primarily are responses to the behaviors of the other person.

7. Unconscious messages exist in all stories and unconscious processing is an inherent property of the human mind. You are aware of only a small fraction of what you are experiencing when you operate solely on the basis of the surface exchange of messages, but you have it all if you also trigger decode the narratives with which you are confronted and tap into the realm of unconscious experience.

We have garnered a sense of what dreams and narratives are about. It's time now to develop the specific ways we can access their deep meanings and intelligence so we can be masters of our fates instead of victims of forces within and around us of which we know nothing.

Part II

TRIGGER DECODING

Chapter 5

Holding on to Dreams

We've been introduced to dreams, stories and triggers. We've tried to get a feeling for how they're designed and structured and how these entities come together to reveal the world of unconscious experience. Part II will concentrate on the details of the decoding process—the trigger decoding method that unlocks the doors to this vast and remarkable world of unconscious power and insight.

We will first concentrate our efforts on dreams. The essential goal we will set is that of beginning with a recent dream and ending with a trigger decoded insight that is truly unexpected and also of great import—fresh knowledge that can make a difference in your life.

As we have seen, there are two basic components which need to be brought together to give us a picture of the realm of unconscious experience: a story line (a narrative vehicle) and its trigger. The pursuit we will carry out is called *processing a dream* because dreams are our starting point. Nevertheless, while the dream is the starting point in our search for insight, in the life of the dreamer the trigger actually came *first* and the dream *second*, as a response to the trigger. This means that ultimately, we'll be working to *process* the trigger event or more precisely, to capture how the mind of the dreamer unconsciously processed that event.

It is not dreams that so much affects our lives,
but their triggers.

We process a dream in order to extract through trigger decoding its most compelling secret messages. We are not especially interested in analyzing a surface dream, as we are in processing it. While we do pause to examine the surface contents of a dream, there's a far richer treasure of knowledge buried in the depths of a dream. So while we do indulge in a bit of analyzing upon hearing a surface dream, we mainly use the surface as a fountainhead or as a source of additional *associations* and *themes*.

> *The greatest value of a surface dream lies with its power to evoke associations to its images or elements. For this reason we call a remembered dream an* origination narrative—*it is the point of origin for the guided associations that provide the themes needed to bring us into the depths of human experience.*

Dreams serve us best as sources of what are called *guided associations* (associations that are evoked by the elements of a dream rather than freely generated as the mind dictates). The kind of guided associations that serve us best are fresh stories, narratives that come to mind as the dreamer allows a dream element to suggest associations, memories and events of any kind, personal or otherwise.

> *In working with a dream, we attempt to build as much narrative imagery as possible because stories are the language of the deep unconscious mind.*

DREAMS AND THEIR ASSOCIATIONS

We want to concentrate now on two issues: first, the means by which we can best insure that we'll remember a dream long enough to process it (when time permits), and second, identifying the kinds of dreams that have the strength and potential to evoke meaningful guided associations and, ultimately, to reveal something important if processed properly—identifying so-called *power dreams*.

Let's develop these points in the context of a better grasp of the process we're engaging in. We are seeking to maximize storied communication because narratives are the main mode of communication used by the deep unconscious system—the great unconscious processing system of the human mind.

As we saw, the story in a surface dream is about one thing, but the dream has been created to condense into its imagery stories about several other things, the trigger events. The surface dream may be about virtually anything, but the unconscious story is about a current trigger. Similarly, the guided associations to a dream should be storied in nature, and when they take that form, they are a rich source of new thematic threads and power. As we will see, these associated stories can range far and wide, but their encoded meanings always pertain to a currently active trigger event.

> *Dreams are the means through which we build a thematic or narrative pool, a* dream associational network *or a collection of encoded themes that can be linked to their triggers.*

To offer a brief example, Nell dreams she is standing on a beach.

QUESTION 5.1

What can you surmise from the surface contents of this dream as it stands by itself?

Answer 5.1

We would have to say very little. The surface dream is quite devoid of detectable meaning. What could beach mean? Does Nell want to be at the beach? Does she live near one? Has something happened at one? The dream raises far more questions than it answers. Even with a more complex surface dream, the yield is typically thin.

To continue with our vignette, through guided associating, Nell recalls a time in her childhood when she lost her parents on a beach.

Question 5.2

What does this guided association add to your understanding of the dream and Nell?

Answer 5.2

Again, the yield in meaning is thin. The association offers one fresh theme, that of loss. This gives us a clue but not a solution; Nell must be working over something that happened that entailed a loss of some kind. That something must, of course, be the trigger event for her dream. As yet, we have no way of knowing what that event was.

Question 5.3

As an exercise in using *themes to suggest triggers*, can you think of some possible triggers for this dream and its guided association? Remember, the nature of the trigger must fit with the nature of the themes.

Any answer you made that involved loss of some kind would be correct. The loss theme is so barren for the moment, that you have almost no clue to the type of loss Nell has suffered. It could be anything from the death of someone to the loss of a relationship, job, body part or whatever.

The beach is a second but far more indefinite clue; it could refer to a current setting such as a beach, vacation site and such, but it's hard to specify a trigger event on the basis of the surface dream alone.

The actual answer in this case was that the dream and its association encoded Nell's *unconscious* perception and realization that her husband was being unfaithful to her. The affair had begun when Nell and her husband had vacationed at the beach.

The bridging themes, then, that go from the dream-associational network to the trigger event are beach and loss. Both themes can be found in the pool of themes and the trigger experience, even though Nell was consciously unaware of the situation. Still, the unconscious perception did affect her behavior and she was very difficult with her husband and had been flirting with her boss at work.

The evolved design of the human mind defensively and automatically keeps Nell from directly realizing her unconscious perceptions of her husband—they exist outside of her awareness. However, the mind does have the facility for encoding these unconscious realizations, condensing, displacing and disguising them within a dream and its guided associations.

In this instance, Nell dreamt a seemingly innocuous surface dream of standing on a beach. The dream itself did not offer a detectable clue to Nell's real life, adaptive issue. However, the guided association pointed more clearly to the trigger event via the memory of losing her parents. The theme of the lost parents encodes or disguises the theme of the lost husband. But it's only when we know the trigger for Nell's dream-associational network that we can properly and meaningfully decode Nell's disguised imagery. The story from her childhood camouflages a story from her present life.

As you can see again, with the dream alone, we'd have almost nothing to say about Nell except that she was thinking about a beach while she slept. With the addition of this particular guided association, all we could add is that she seems to feel lost in some way. But with both the guided association and the trigger, we have a story we can put together, a story about Nell and her husband encoded in a story about Nell and her parents.

With few exceptions, the associations to a dream are more powerful and meaningful than the dream itself.

The more powerful the themes of a surface dream, the greater the likelihood you'll generate strong, guided associations to that dream and produce a deeply meaningful thematic pool. We want, then, to learn how to remember our dreams and how to keep them in mind for later processing, especially if the dream is a strong one.

FIXING A DREAM IN YOUR MIND

Self-processing or *dream processing* begins, of course, with remembering a dream, one valuable type of origination narrative. All dreams are not created equal. They vary considerably in their surface contents and in their potential to serve as points of departure for meaningful guided associations. It is well to learn how to recognize a promising dream—its attributes and potential. On the other hand, every dream, no matter how seemingly trivial on the surface, has the potential to set off a series of strong guided associations.

You should try to process every dream you can remember.

Left to chance and to human nature, we tend to forget our dreams as the day wears on. We need time to process a dream, and there are few opportunities during the day to properly work with a dream and its triggers. For most people, before going to sleep seems to be a propitious time for the processing effort. Other good times for processing a dream are during solitary activities that take little or no thought, such as riding on a bus or train, driving a car, or a long break from work and other responsibilities.

However, the ideal processing opportunity occurs in the morning upon awakening from a night's sleep. Most dreams are remembered at that time (although some are recalled in the course of the day). If you can arrange it, it's best to recall the dream as you wake up and to process it at the same time—an effort that takes anywhere from 30 to 45 minutes. This should be done while you are alone because others only interfere with what must be a personal and private processing effort. Simply stay in bed and do your processing there by yourself. While you might want a cup of coffee to help you along, dream processing should be done with thought alone and without other satisfactions for the moment.

In processing a dream, nothing should be written down—dreams are part of a natural process that is greatly disturbed by record making of any kind. Forgetting dreams is as important as their recall. If you don't recall a dream for processing, you always can make up a story and go from there.

Despite the many objections to this constraint, if you're pursuing deeply unconscious wisdom, you must make a spontaneous unrecorded effort. Most people who write down their dreams tend to engage in the so-called analysis of their surface contents. They do not work with their triggers; they place their dreams in the rather barren world of conscious experience and divorce them from the immediate and specific issues of their lives which trigger decoding could help them illuminate. Their written dreams are more like relics than living specimens.

Self-processing usually begins with a remembered dream. Let's now deal with the issue of capturing a dream.

QUESTION 5.4

As far as you know, what are some of the ways you can try to insure remembering as much of your dreams as possible?

ANSWER 5.4

There are several ways to maximize your chances of remembering your dreams. Here is a list.

1. On awakening, linger in bed and allow your mind to ignore the realities of your life—past, present, and future. Think only about your dreams and pursue their recall both actively and passively, searching for dream fragments and also allowing them to come into your relaxed mind. Plunging into the tasks and

issues of everyday reality activates the conscious system and its focused thinking and adaptations; staying out of the flow of your life for a few minutes will facilitate dream recall.

2. Once remembered, mark a dream mentally, but, again *do not write down any part of the dream.* A dream is a living entity, a way of coping; allow it to live and breathe. Writing down a dream extrudes it from your mind and detaches it from yourself; it moves the working-over of a dream outside of your mind and it deadens the dream's mental connections and active meanings. And there are no excuses for writing down a dream; if they are lost, you can always go with a made-up story.

3. If you are not going to process your dream on the spot, associate briefly to its different elements. A few guided associations will help to anchor the dream in your memory for later processing.

4. Mark as many of the powerful themes in your dream-associational network you can identify. Create an image of your dream that stresses these power themes.

5. Think of the possible triggers for your dream. Making a mental note of the key triggers for a dream tends to facilitate recalling the dream itself later on: triggers and dream themes are made of the same cloth.

6. Pausing from time to time during the day to recall your dreams—their power themes and triggers—will help keep the dream alive and available until it can be processed.

Mark your dreams mentally without fear of losing them, reassured that if you forget everything you dreamt during a given night, you can make up a story and process the story as your dream.

EXERCISE

Over the next few days make a deliberate effort each morning to hold on to your dreams. When you wake up the first morning, let nature take its course. Try to remember your dreams and once you do, let them slide into the back of your mind. Make no effort to think about them during the day and then at night, when alone, try to recall as much of your dreams as you can. Notice whether you remembered most or all of your dreams, and if you lost a fair amount or everything. This is your first pass at dream recall, try to get a sense of how it went.

The next morning, linger in bed and try out the methods of fixing the recall of dreams described above. That night, again attempt to remember your dreams. Compare the results of these two methods of capturing your dreams. As a rule, your more systematic efforts should enhance dream recall. In addition, you should be able to detect your own personal issues in dream recall and identify what you need to do to make remembering dreams work for you.

Develop your own memory techniques for marking dream elements and themes. Never dismiss a remembered dream as too simple, weak, or inconsequential. As we saw with Nell, some of the barest dreams can evoke strong and significant guided associations.

With your dream in mind, we turn now to the issue of the good dream—the question of power in dream material.

Chapter 6

Power in Dreams

The unconscious part of the human mind processes images, meanings, and aspects of events that are unbearable to awareness. These impingements are automatically perceived unconsciously or subliminally, entirely without conscious registration and then, as noted, processed unconsciously as well. The intensity of these issues introduces the concept of *power* into the process of decoding dreams.

> *The essential proposition is that dreams reflect the unconscious processing of powerful emotional impingements and concerns, and this power must be captured and encoded in the themes in the surface dream and in the guided associations to the dream.*

We can anticipate the main themes of this chapter:

1. Dreams and their guided associations encode images and themes that are extremely disturbing to the conscious mind. The issues that are encoded in dreams are very strong and difficult.
2. This indicates that a meaningful and cogent collation of the themes in the surface dream and the dream-associational network must reflect the disturbing power of the underlying issues that they deal with. Meaningful insight therefore can arise only when there are a sufficient number of power themes available for linking to and characterizing the unconscious

experience of their trigger events. Power is an essential feature of a workable dream-associational network.

3. The definition of power themes becomes quite important for effective trigger decoding: no power, no compelling realization; with power, deep understanding is feasible.

For ease of discussion, let's use the term *dream* to refer collectively to both the surface dream itself and the storied guided associations that arise from thinking about the elements of the dream—*the dream-associational network or pool of themes,* the collection of encoded thematic material we need for linking with and giving meaning to their trigger events. Themes give insight into trigger events; they bridge from the surface to the depths.

We've identified ways of ensnaring our dreams. The question we are now addressing is: how do we know we have a potentially valuable dream on our hands, what we might call a good or promising dream?

> *Strong surface dream themes tend to generate strong guided associations and lead to meaningful, deep insights.*

This implies that strong surface dream themes speak for highly workable dreams. With that proposition in mind, let's seek out the specific signs of power in the themes in a dream. An exercise will help us to find our way.

EXERCISE

DREAM A Agnes dreams that her friend Paul is standing in the doorway of her kitchen. He leaves and her friend Ellie looks in but she soon leaves in search of Paul.

DREAM B Ben dreams that he's on a bridge. The elevation of the bridge frightens him. He sees a car coming toward him and a man aims a gun at him from the passenger-side window and starts shooting at him. His arm is hit and he begins to bleed, but he finds that he can fly and that he's able to lift himself up from the bridge and escape the gunfire. He floats around for a while, but then suddenly finds himself in a dark room without windows, lit only by candlelight. He is meditating when a woman comes uninvited into the room. She is naked from the waist up. The woman motions toward a bed in the room and asks Ben to make love to her.

DREAM C Lois dreams that she's in a park jogging. It's late afternoon and she has a sense that someone is following her. She looks behind her and sees two menacing looking teenage boys. They are catching up with her. She tries to run faster but they're getting closer. A man sees what's going on and chases the boys away. A car driving in the park goes through a red light. Lois looks around and discovers that she's no longer in the park, but in a classroom. The teacher is a tall woman with dark hair. The lesson is on animal intelligence. Sitting next to Lois is a plump woman of about fifty years of age. When she looks at the woman's face, Lois realizes that the woman is her mother. The woman asks Lois for a cigarette and Lois says she's stopped smoking. A man sitting behind them gives the woman a small cigar, which she lights and begins to puff on. The smoke is choking Lois and she's having trouble breathing, but, suddenly, to her surprise, she discovers that she's outside in the fresh air, in the courtyard of an old house. It is dark and an elderly woman is looking out of one of the windows. A funeral procession awkwardly passes through the courtyard. Lois leaves the courtyard and finds herself in a beautiful meadow where she lies down to rest. Nearby she can hear the sound of a brook and the song of some birds. She falls asleep but the sleep is disrupted by a violent fight between two boys.

QUESTION 6.1

Let's begin our exploration with a basic question: for each of these dreams, indicate whether it is storied (narrative) or nonstoried (nonnarrative) in form.

ANSWER 6.1

Each of these dreams is indeed narrative in form. Each presents a story and describes events, real or imagined. None of these dreams is restricted to analyzing or explaining. Recall that this implies that each dream is a double-meaning communication; each is an *encoded vehicle* that conveys in disguised form a variety of reactions to a series of emotionally charged trigger events.

QUESTION 6.2

Turning now to the issue of *emotional power*, what kinds of themes do you think would reflect strong emotional issues? Strong themes indicate strong triggers and equally strong unconscious perceptions. Another way of asking this question is, what do you think are the most compelling kinds of unconscious experiences in emotional life?

Answer 6.2

Years of work with dreams have shown that there are a limited number of truly powerful emotional issues in our daily lives. These issues are reflected in themes that virtually always indicate powerful, emotionally charged triggers and responsive unconscious perceptions. These encoded themes appear in a surface dream because they have been displaced or removed from the trigger event and situated elsewhere, in some other (surface) setting. Thus, the connection between a theme and its trigger is broken.

> *The theme is taken from the trigger event and relocated elsewhere. But the unconscious experience, which is reflected in the disguised theme, is still there; it is conveyed in encoded form.*
>
> *In processing a dream, we begin with the themes and search for their evocative trigger events, reversing what happened in reality where the trigger event has evoked the encoded thematic response.*

Every meaningful pool of themes will contain one or more power themes. The list of power themes includes:

SEXUALITY Overt, explicitly sexual themes in a surface dream or story speaks for strong underlying issues. The allusion must be open and direct: intercourse, nudity, sexual seduction, oral sex. While Freud certainly overstated the case for the role of sexuality in human emotional life, he nevertheless touched on an issue that to some extent creates emotional conflict for everyone. There are many sources of sexual imagery in unconscious processing; the trigger need not be overtly sexual. For example, whenever a rule, law, or frame is broken—by someone coming uninvited into a class you are attending or someone breaking into your house—the intrusion will be experienced unconsciously as sexually tinged. And the sexualized experience is valid and will unconsciously determine what you do and feel.

Remember that the world of unconscious experience is far different from that of conscious experience.

QUESTION 6.3

Where is the sexual imagery in these dreams?

ANSWER 6.3

The only overt sexual allusions in these dreams are in Dream B, reflected in the image of the woman who is naked from the waist up and her request to Ben that he make love to her. The menacing boys in Dream C, with the suggestive quality of possible rape, is *not* an overtly, undisguised sexual image. On the whole, then, these dreams are sparse in respect to sexual power.

THEMES OF DEATH, INJURY, ILLNESS, HARM, AND ASSAULT   This is a collection of grim and traumatic themes (the Damage Group of Themes) that virtually always speak for powerful triggers and unconscious perceptions. Remember again that whatever the surface image, the theme also is encoding a response to a repressed trigger event; something has unconsciously activated perceptions of being injured, attacked or annihilated. The themes must prompt a search for the missing trigger event so the unconscious experience is properly understood.

QUESTION 6.4

Identify as many death and damage themes as you can in the three dreams previously presented.

ANSWER 6.4

There are no damage themes in the first dream. In Dream B, the damage themes are the individual being shot at, being wounded, and bleeding. Dream C has a qualified damage theme in the menacing boys and in Lois' inability to breathe and a clear damage theme in the fight between the boys. The funeral procession is, of course, an allusion to death.

EVENTS THAT ARE UNLIKELY OR IMPOSSIBLE IN REALITY Unrealistic happenings are not uncommon in dreams. Generally, they are looked upon as one of the unusual characteristics of dreams and thought of as reflecting the dream's lack of contact with reality. However, we've already seen that decoded dreams and the unconscious experiences they convey are exquisitely in touch with reality, even more so than most conscious emotional experiences and beliefs.

Unrealistic events in dreams draw their importance from the finding that, as a rule, they are signs of severe unconscious anxiety related to a strange and disquieting trigger event. When those we love or interact with have unexpectedly hurt us emotionally when we expect kindness and support, or when their behaviors are self-contradictory (saying one thing and doing another, giving out one message and then emitting its very opposite), we perceive a contrariness in them and often sense they are driving us a bit crazy as well.

These are, I assure you, extremely common feelings and not at all a sign of emotional disturbance. Each of has an inner core of contradictions and each of us expresses ourselves in maddening ways to others. Still, the intensity of the anxieties that underlie these unrealistic images often is so great that they tend to be difficult to associate to—we dread where they will take us. Nevertheless, these images are markers of strong triggers and need to be associated to and pursued as such.

QUESTION 6.5

Identify as many unrealistic images as you can in these three dreams.

ANSWER 6.5

As with the other categories, Dream A is lacking in this type of power imagery. Ben's flying in Dream B is, of course, impossible in reality. Although it is not an uncommon image, dreams of flying are indications of strong underlying issues and should be subjected to guided associations. In addition, Ben's sudden shift from flying to an enclosed room cannot happen in reality.

In Dream C, the shift from the park to the classroom is a sudden change that also could not happen in reality, as is the later sequence in which Lois mysteriously finds herself no longer in the smoke filled room and unexpectedly in a courtyard. Finally, the funeral procession passing through the courtyard also qualifies as highly unlikely. Whether it is conceivable or not, it is a surface dream element that should attract several guided associations.

ALLUSIONS TO BOUNDARIES AND FRAMES, SUCH AS LAWS AND RULES The conscious system pays little attention to a group of themes and emotional concerns to which the deep unconscious system is extremely sensitive. This refers to issues of rules, laws, boundaries, and frames. Our general unfamiliarity with this important group of themes is a reflection of the conscious mind's relative insensitivity to this aspect of our lives. However, everything we do in life is framed in some type of setting or context, including life itself which is, as you know, framed by death. Relationships also unfold within a framework, that with a parent is one frame and that with a spouse or lover quite another.

Emotional life is organized and deeply affected by ground rules, laws, frames, and boundaries. They set the tone for everything we do and every situation in which we do it. There are ideal settings, rules, and boundaries for the family situation, schooling, earning a living, and each of the major areas of activity in our lives. The law of the land is a statement of rules, as is the necessary interpersonal boundaries between parents and children, students and teachers, and bosses and their employees.

The conscious system ignores rules and tends to be cavalier about adhering to them, preferring, in most instances, to modify or break a rule rather than obey it. This rule-breaking propensity reflects wishes for omnipotent power, denial of helplessness and death, and other costly defenses that nevertheless are preferred by the conscious mind when faced with adhering to stated and unstated tenets.

In sharp contrast, the deep unconscious system strongly prefers the security and strength-giving attributes of adhering to ground rules, laws, frames, and boundaries. The system appreciates the curative and personally enhancing powers of secured rather than altered or deviant frames.

> *The deep unconscious system is highly sensitive to frame-related triggers and has a strong respect for the power of frames to affect our lives.*
> *Our encoded themes consistently favor secured or ideal rules, frames, and boundaries.*

Frame-related themes are evoked by frame-related triggers; they are always a sign of power. Examples of secured frame themes (adhering to ground rules) are obeying rules and laws, such as a parent's keeping personal secrets from their children, maintaining privacy and confidentiality when called for, and creating a safe home space within which a child can grow and flourish.

Examples of frame-modifying or frame-breaking themes include all criminal acts, lying, and cheating; for example, a parent who enters their child's bedroom without knocking on its closed door, or someone publically revealing their private secrets. In a dream-associational network, these are power themes that have been evoked by strong frame-related triggers, and they should elicit guided associations.

QUESTION 6.6

Identify as many allusions to rules, laws, frames, and boundaries as you can in this dream material.

Answer 6.6

Dream A is again weak in frame power. At most, the allusions to the doorway and kitchen refer to physical frames, but these are meager allusions.

Dream B has physical frames such as the bridge, car, window, and room. The law is broken by the person who is shooting at Ben, while boundaries are violated by the woman who comes uninvited into his room. Her partial nudity also modifies a usual boundary, that of clothing.

Dream C has the physical frames of the park, car, classroom, courtyard, and meadow. Other allusions to rules and boundaries include the boys who are invading Lois' interpersonal space, the car that goes through the red light thereby breaking a law, the fight between the boys which suggests a violation of the necessary distance between two people, and the funeral procession that alludes to death, which is the boundary condition for life.

Exercise

Over the next few days, make careful note of how you and the people with whom you have contact deal with ground rules, laws, and boundaries. Catalog the types of frame issues you've observed. Think through the precise nature of the ideal or secured ground rules and frames of the situations in which you find yourself. Notice how often these issues arise, and how often rules are adhered to, and how often they are broken.

You are likely to be surprised at how ubiquitous this dimension is; everything you do has a frame (or sorely lacks one). You probably will begin to notice that rules or frames often are broken and far more rarely adhered to. But you'll be helping yourself if you become acquainted with one of the most important and neglected aspects of human life and living—the context around which almost all unconscious experience is organized.

DREAMS OF EARLY CHILDHOOD INCIDENTS OR SIGNIFICANT FIGURES Often, allusions to notable childhood figures or incidents, whether in the surface dream or the guided associations, speak for strong underlying issues. In general, these images suggest that something traumatic is happening in the present that in some way replicates an early childhood trauma. The appearance of these early childhood figures promises to facilitate the development of connections between current trigger events and the early life of the dreamer.

QUESTION 6.7

Where in these dreams is there a reference to an early childhood incident or figure?

ANSWER 6.7

An early childhood figure appears in only one dream, Dream C, in which Lois dreams of her mother. Guided associations to her mother should prove productive.

POWER VERSUS EMOTIONAL CONCERNS

It is likely that you've wondered about the absence on this list of a number of themes you'd tend to think of as powerful. For example, there's the universal concern with separation and loss, the endless problems most people have with money and finances, pregnancy and birth, issues of self-esteem and control, and emotions such as anxiety and guilt.

To clarify this issue, two distinctions must be made.

The first is that there is a great difference between an emotional concern and a power theme.

The topics I've just alluded to touch on emotional concerns, but they do not reflect encoded and unconscious power. When something concerns you emotionally, it will function as a trigger event, but the *power* of the experience will be conveyed in the power themes identified in this chapter. The loss of a loved one takes on power as a damage theme, money issues often involve rules and frames, pregnancy touches on overt sexuality and concerns about damage physically. If you settle for these lesser themes in your dream-associational network, you will not bother to generate the power themes you need for linking up with active trigger events.

The second distinction involves understanding the sensitivities of the conscious mind as compared to those of the unconscious mind; they are very different.

The conscious mind tends to be self-protective in the emotional realm. It uses frame breaks to protect itself from unbearable realizations of helplessness, and it generally keeps things ill-defined and as minimally powerful as possible so its survival functions will operate smoothly. Issues like self-control, controlling others, and self-esteem or self-image are emotionally important topics for the conscious mind, but they do not concern the unconscious mind unless they connect to more powerful conflicts and concerns. The conscious mind tends to be occupied with intellectual issues which lack deep power; the unconscious mind moves along power tracts only.

QUESTION 6.8

Let's consider the overall power of the three dreams we've been working with. Which of these dreams has the most and least power? Explain the basis for your answer.

ANSWER 6.8

Dream A is certainly the weakest of the three dreams; it does not have a single powerful element in its surface contents. It is a dream that is unlikely to generate strong guided associations, a situation that calls for a generating a *supplementary origination narrative* (a made-up story or a waking dream) to beef up the pool of themes.

Dream B has about five major power themes: the shooting, being wounded, flying, partial nudity, and sexual intercourse. It is a surface dream with an optimal number of strong themes and is therefore a highly promising dream to respond to with guided associations.

Dream C has three strong elements: the menacing boys, the funeral, and the fight between the boys. It's power is moderate at best, however, because the power themes are not especially compelling. For example, the appearance of a funeral touches on the theme of death, but the emptiness of the image weakens the allusion.

Overall, it is clear, then, that Dream B is the most powerful and promising dream of the three. However, there's more to consider in looking at a surface dream, so let's press on.

Some Other Attributes of Remembered Dreams

To complete this discussion of remembered dreams, let's develop the sense of another important feature of surface dreams. This topic will be approached by asking a question.

Question 6.9

There is an as yet unmentioned consideration in evaluating a surface dream for its potential for developing a meaningful dream-processing exercise. In addition to the areas already explored, can you detect any problems with Dreams A and C? Hint: each has a different problem in the same area.

Answer 6.9

Dream A, which we've already identified as sorely lacking in power imagery, is also problematic because it is relatively brief. A promising dream is long enough to include a sufficient diversity of surface elements in order to allow for a diversity of guided associations; shifting about from one story to another tends to increase the richness and power of the pool of themes.

On the other hand, Dream C is much too long for effective processing. It would be difficult for the dreamer to associate to this dream without getting scattered and confused. The human mind can process only so much information and meaning. Dream C demands more attention and associating than one can be expected to develop. There are far too many dream elements to associate to in the available span of time (about 45 minutes). In addition, there are relatively few strong images in proportion to the length of the dream; nearly the entire dream is made up of bland imagery.

Dream B is basically ideal in its length and in the number of powerful surface images it contains.

Some key points worth pondering are:

1. A moderately long dream is relatively ideal in length for a workable dream. The dream also should include two or more powerful surface images.

2. Too little dream material will usually restrict the richness and variability of the available guided associations; there will be too few themes and a sparseness of power themes to work with.

3. Too many dream elements will make it impossible to associate to each of them and will tend to evoke scattered guided associations and make it difficult to organize the pool of themes into a coherent set of meanings; power themes may be so excessive they cannot be integrated meaningfully with their trigger events.

4. With too few dream elements, create a supplementary origination narrative by making up a short story and associating to it as you would to a dream.

5. With too many dream elements, concentrate your guided associations on the *power images* in the dream; it is well to confine your associations to one dream segment at a time and to not feel a need to associate to every surface image.

Take the most recent dream that you can remember. Memorize the list of power themes offered in this chapter and assess the power of your surface dream. Be sure to search for frame-related themes and don't overlook things that probably or certainly are unlikely to have occurred in reality (we tend to steer away from such images).

Develop one or two guided associations to your dream. Make sure they're stories. Once you've told yourself these tales, assess the power of the themes in these associations. Compare the power of the surface dream and that of the guided associations. In most cases, if you were loose in associating, you will find more power in the guided associations than in the surface dream itself.

EXERCISE

Mentally keep track of your dreams over the next several days. Associate to each dream you remember. Assess the power of each surface dream and compare that with the power of the associations to the dream. Track the total power of your dream-associational networks over the course of several days. Often, power will wax and wane, mounting one day and fading the next. An unrelenting sequence of powerful dreams suggest a lingering powerful trigger issue, one that needs to be subjected to trigger decoding so you can resolve and make peace with the underlying concerns and anxieties.

At this point, hopefully, we've learned how to keep our dreams available for processing and which dreams have the promise of power. Let's turn now to the specific steps though which dreams are processed.

As we proceed, let's keep in mind the maxim that it's not the dream we ultimately need to deal with, but the triggers that have evoked the dream and its themes.

Chapter 7

The Face of the Dream

We are now poised to answer the pivotal question: how do we process our dreams so as to arrive at deep understanding, to discover something important to our emotional lives that we didn't know beforehand? In essence, how do we carry out effective trigger decoding?

The decoding process we will develop in the remainder of the book is composed of the following sequence:

1. Recognizing and getting what you can from the surface dream;
2. generating guided associations to the images or elements of the surface dream;
3. developing a sense of your emotional issues and difficulties, the problems that your dream has a bearing on;
4. identifying the recent trigger events that have had the greatest impact on your unconscious mind;
5. getting a sense of the main qualities and attributes of each triggering event;
6. identifying the most powerful themes in your pool of themes;
7. extracting these themes from their surface story so they are free to be connected to the trigger experience;
8. linking these themes to the key trigger events as a reflection of your unconscious experience

of those events and then defining your unconscious reactions to your unconscious experience;

9. using the insights generated through trigger decoding to clarify your emotional issues and choices and to find optimal solutions to your emotional dilemmas.

In this chapter we will deal mainly with the first of these steps, working with the surface dream.

As has been stressed all along, *analyzing* a surface dream is an appealing but highly defensive and minimally revealing effort. Even though it takes a little work and brings you to realizations you both fear and deeply need, trigger decoding is a far more valuable and helpful process. While the steps in trigger decoding may seem a bit complex, the essence of the process can be simply stated:

> *The key elements in processing a dream can be reduced to developing themes and identifying triggers.*

There's an awesome, deep world in our minds and its communications need to be explored and mastered through themes and triggers—it is well worth the bother. The journey into the depths begins on the surface with the manifest contents of the dream as dreamt and recalled. As we have seen, this is a terrain with a modicum of meaning of its own and with contours that disguise far greater riches beneath their surface. Still, we initiate dream processing with this surface structure, the surface dream.

APPROACHING THE FACE OF THE DREAM

I have downplayed the importance of the surface dream in favor of the use of the dream for guided associations. We will not, however, simply discard the manifest dream. There is some value in having a sense of the meanings and implications of your surface dream images before plunging into guided associating and the pursuit of unconscious experience.

In this chapter we will define what the face of a dream can tell you and what it cannot tell you as well.

In approaching the surface of the dream we should, then, be mindful of both its value and its limitations. The human mind is naturally designed to avoid deep unconscious meanings. We therefore need to keep reminding ourselves to be wary of the natural inclination to limit ourselves to facile readings of the surface of a dream in the mistaken belief that we've learned something deeply significant.

We must be mindful that the surface dream is largely connected to the conscious mind and that what it reveals is largely familiar territory, however surprising or seemly helpful. No matter how fascinating this reading of the surface may be, there's something far more serious and important underneath. As I've often stated, the most compelling functions of a dream are to evoke guided associations and to encode unconscious perceptions and messages. Let's not settle for less.

We can make use of the face of a dream in several ways.

BY UNDERSTANDING THE SURFACE MESSAGE There is, of course, meaning in the surface story of a dream. Although directly stated and conscious, it's worth knowing. It is therefore of value to go through a reading of the surface and grasp its main meanings and their implications. Even though this is an effort laced with surprisingly strong defensiveness and avoidance, it can tell you things about conscious issues and conflicts you may not have had in focus. Sometimes there even are clues as to how to resolve these problems.

BY IDENTIFYING THE MANIFEST THEMES The remaining explorations of a surface dream bridge from its surface to its encoded depths. The first of these examinations is carried out to answer the question of just how much power—how many *power themes*—the dream contains.

The themes in a surface dream are also part of your pool of themes, part of the thematic resource (encoded meanings) you need for linking up with your triggers. Going over the surface themes in a dream gives you a sense of both its evident meanings and its potential as a source of unconscious meaning and guided associations.

BY IDENTIFYING THE FRAME-RELATED THEMES Recall that the deep unconscious system is exceedingly sensitive to frames, such as rules, laws, and boundaries. In fact, all of our emotional issues and conflicts are worked over in the unconscious realm in frame-related terms.

The frame is like the hub of a wheel and our emotional issues fan out from that center. All of the dynamic conflicts we are concerned with—those related to sexuality, aggression, identity and the like—have a *basic frame component*. Thus, assessing the extent of frame-related imagery gives you an idea of the frame-power of a dream and the kind of ground-rule concerns you may be dealing with consciously and especially unconsciously.

> *Monitoring the status of your frame-related imagery is always informative. It's well to know where you and those around you stand when it comes to rules and boundaries.*

SOME LIMITATIONS OF SURFACE MESSAGES

We should confine ourselves to a fairly quick look at the evident meanings of the face of a dream. There's no point in dwelling on the surface for three main reasons:

1. Your impressions of the surface are likely to be *personally biased* and therefore difficult to learn from. Defensiveness is the primary commitment of the conscious mind in the emotional realm. Decoding a dream requires overriding these expedient, but also costly, protective needs so we can delve into the important realm of unconscious experience and wisdom.
2. The surface meanings tend to echo things you already know and therefore are unlikely to tell you anything genuinely new or startling.
3. There's a lot of work to be done in processing a dream toward unconscious meaning. The longer you dwell on the surface, the less time you have for the processing effort and the harder it will be for you to shift into the decoding mode and to sustain the search for decoded insight.

With these warnings in mind, let's get a feeling for the kinds of things that nevertheless can be gleaned from a surface dream.

EXERCISE

Jan dreams that she goes into her bedroom and finds her sister, Meg, in bed with her husband, Mark. Meg runs out of the bedroom and Mark hides under the covers. When Jan pulls away the covers the man is not her husband but Arthur, a teacher at the school where Jan teaches. Arthur's face is swollen and red; he appears to be febrile and very ill. He asks Jan to call a doctor and she begins to cry. She goes to the phone to call her gynecologist, but realizes that's the wrong doctor to call. She stands there puzzled, not knowing what to do, and the dream ends.

What can you find in the way of surface meaning in this dream?

ANSWER 7.1

Surface dreams yield a set of *directly dramatized themes*. On the whole, they tend to reflect conscious concerns as they are worked over in direct dream imagery. They may illuminate an aspect of a problem that had escaped your notice or give you a lead to a solution to a dilemma you had missed. But mainly they illustrate and deal with *known* current problems and issues.

You can organize the surface contents of your dreams in terms of the following:

- the setting
- the people, who they are, the picture of yourself and others
- the nature of the main action
- evident conflicts
- other concerns and issues, the themes of the dream
- coping strategies and solutions to problems and their success or failure
- feelings or emotions

These are straightforward categories and they capture the main qualities of a manifest dream. Knowing what the surface dream contains can be illuminating and of some help with your emotional issues, but it's well to remember that you're looking at a small part of your emotional world and by no means the most important part. You're limited to the figures and settings in the dream itself; you have no way of identifying the more crucial displaced or disguised meanings of these same images.

EXERCISE
Review Jan's dream and answer the following questions about its surface contents.

QUESTION 7.2
Identify the setting of Jan's dream. What kinds of issues does the setting suggest? Be conservative in your speculations.

ANSWER 7.2
The setting is Jan's bedroom which suggests sexual concerns, a point elaborated on in the subsequent imagery of the dream.

QUESTION 7.3
Who populates the dream? What does their presence suggest to you?

ANSWER 7.3

The figures in the dream are Jan, her sister, her husband, and Arthur, a fellow teacher. Jan's gynecologist is mentioned but she does not appear in the surface dream imagery. It is difficult to know what these people are doing in Jan's dream. The best guess is that she's concerned about something related to her sister and husband, but why Arthur and her gynecologist are in the dream is a mystery. While the action of the dream clarifies the presence of some of these people, it also cries out for some guided associations that would elaborate on the underlying reasons they are there.

QUESTION 7.4

What is the nature of the main action in the dream? Again, what could it imply or mean?

ANSWER 7.4

The action of the dream begins with Jan discovering her sister and husband together in bed. The sister flees and the husband hides and is then transformed into Arthur who is ill. There is the request for help, Jan's tears, her mistakenly beginning to call her gynecologist for help for a man, and then not knowing what to do.

This summary of the action line simply reiterates what appears to be the main drama of the dream. Suggesting underlying meanings for this sequence of events would be highly speculative. We would tend to repeat the description of the events and suggest that there probably is indeed some evident concern about what's going on between Jan's sister and her husband, the use of flight from a disturbing situation, and something about Arthur and about illness. Does Jan have a gynecological problem, we might wonder, and why does she feel so helpless? It would be all but impossible to answer these questions.

Formulations of the surface contents of dreams are far more uncertain, personally biased, and open to defensive pressures than the process of trigger decoding the same dream. Oddly, then, it's easier to determine the unconscious adaptive meanings of a dream than it is to understand its surface meanings.

QUESTION 7.5

What are the evident conflicts and main concerns or themes of the dream? What might they imply or mean?

ANSWER 7.5

We have already answered much of this question. Jan seems likely to be in conflict with her sister and husband, and concerned with incest, infidelity, betrayal, illness, and getting medical care. It seems too uncertain to try to guess what this all amounts to. Again, we feel a need for guided associations.

QUESTION 7.6

What are Jan's coping strategies and how successful are they?

Jan's seems to be coping first with betrayal, then infidelity and incest, by discovering a problem between her sister and husband. The discovery leads to flight and the escape response may well reflect Jan's own way of dealing with emotionally charged issues. Finally, there is the need to cope with illness and Jan is unable to do so. There is a distinct failure at coping.

QUESTION 7.7

What feelings or emotions appear in the dream?

ANSWER 7.7

The only expressed emotion is found in Jan's crying. The meaning of this act is uncertain. It's difficult to know if she's depressed, frustrated, or over-involved with Arthur.

To summarize, in looking over a surface dream, try to make sense of its direct and implied messages. This means that you should try to weave an emotionally relevant story from its evident themes in order to allow it to direct your thinking about your emotional concerns in a way that will afford them illumination.

On the basis of this dream, we could overall suggest that Jan may be experiencing some kind of sexual conflict in her marriage or that she may be worried about an attraction between her husband and sister. We would wonder why Arthur appears in the dream and speculate that he may be coming on to Jan or that she's attracted to him. And why, we'd ask, does illness come up, and what about calling a gynecologist to see Arthur, or being unable to find help for him. Finally, there is Jan's crying, a sign of depression or distress, which is somehow tied to illness, although we can't be certain of its possible deeper sources.

Surface dreams seldom tell a well integrated or complete story. They are like fragmented clues. Manifest dreams seldom reveal answers to our emotionally charged mysteries. It's usually difficult to put the picture together into a whole and satisfying insight.

Of course, Jan knows what's going on in her life, so she can connect to her dream. Let's see what learning something about Jan's life will tell us about the surface dream.

In reality, Jan has seen no sign of seduction or excessive interest between her husband and sister. Does this mean that Jan has missed something consciously while *awake* and that she's giving herself a clue consciously while *asleep* (surface dreams are conscious rather than unconscious communications). Alerted to this possibility, Jan might watch her sister and husband more closely to see if her dream reflects a realization she had missed while awake. Or does the dream simply reflect a disguised fantasy or wish of Jan's?

In regard to illness, Jan is worried about her father who is getting on in years and had had a heart attack a year earlier. He looked thin and pale the last time she saw him and she had wondered if he had a hidden cancer. This links up with the image of Arthur lying ill; not being able to get him a doctor ties in with Jan's feeling that her father's doctor isn't helping him and her feeling helpless to do anything about it. Jan had suggested another physician to her father, but he had refused to change doctors.

As you can see, the surface dream weaves nicely into a fabric of sorts with the consciously known events and concerns of Jan's life. She's alerted to look a bit more closely at the relationship between her husband and sister, to think more about why Arthur would show up in her dream, and to intensify her concerns about her father's health.

It's a neat package and we sense some meaning. In fact, if we took the dream no further, we'd feel we'd accomplished something through this analysis and synthesis, and we'd have no way of knowing how much more the dream contained. This is why it has been noted that working over surface dreams is relatively easy, interesting, somewhat productive, and helpful, but limited and defensive.

PREPARING FOR DEEPER PROBES: THEMES

> *The remaining responses to a surface dream are geared toward moving into its condensed, displaced, and disguised meanings.*

However, these pursuits are revealing in themselves, each is a kind of way-station on the road to deeper meaning.

> *The first of these efforts involves picking out the main themes in the surface dream.*

We did something like that in exploring the surface dream for possible meaning. But the kind of thematic sweep we take now is done with a critical question in mind: *what could these themes have to do with triggers, what could have set these themes into action*? That is, we identify themes not so much for their inherent meanings, but as *clues to triggers*.

This approach to themes entails a shift from the direct, conscious world we live in, where a theme is a theme is a theme, to the more indirect and convoluted unconscious world where a theme is something other than it seems to be on the surface and is always connected to a trigger.

> *In the first world, a theme is there to directly reveal a problem, while in the second world, a theme is there to mirror a trigger and to disguise or encode a reaction to that trigger.*

Our framework and ways of thinking are very different, depending on which world we wish to enter and work over.

QUESTION 7.8

What are the main themes in this dream? What kinds of triggers do they suggest? Make the best guess you can.

ANSWER 7.8

In sequence, the main themes are being in a bedroom, the sister and husband being in bed, incest, betrayal, flight, hiding, covering up, change in person, fellow teacher, illness, women's doctor, wrong doctor, not being able to find the right doctor, and being unable to get help.

As for the kinds of triggers they suggest, at this juncture our answer can be only a rather general one. We'd wonder if something's happened in Jan's life to raise the issues of betrayal, inappropriate sexual liaisons, and illness and an inability to get much-needed help.

On the encoded level, dreams reflect and encode reality, not isolated fantasies or inner concerns. There may well be an encoded perception here of some kind of inappropriate contact between Meg and Mel. And there may be something more, something unconscious, in Jan's worries about her father. Or it may be that subliminally Jan has detected an illness in someone else close to her.

To continue this exercise, let's suppose we played back these themes and suggested these triggers to Jan in order to see if they help her to get in touch with a missing trigger. She responds by saying that nothing new or important occurs to her. For the moment, then, all we can do is keep these themes in mind so we can return to them after we've processed Jan's dream for encoded contents.

POWER THEMES

Having established the general run of the themes, we next identify the power themes in the dream. Frequently, there's an overabundance of themes in a surface dream and we need some way to focus our exploration. This selectivity, while it may be used for defensive purposes and must be checked out repeatedly, enables us to concentrate our efforts on major areas of concern and meaning.

QUESTION 7.9

What are the power themes in Jan's dream? How ideal is this dream in respect to power?

ANSWER 7.9

The sexual themes of two people in bed together and of incest are the first of Jan's power themes. There also are themes of betrayal and illness, doctors, the unreal image of the change of the figure of Mark into that of Arthur, and the unlikely thought of calling a gynecologist to take care of Arthur. In all, then, this is a powerful dream with ample power themes.

The themes and triggers we suggested to Jan touched on these power images. They have not as yet jarred loose an evocative trigger from Jan, so again we must await further developments. We can think of these thematic threads as six power themes in search of their trigger.

QUESTION 7.10

We move on to our last search of the surface dream: the quest for themes of rules, laws, frames, and boundaries. What then are the main *frame-related themes* in this dream?

ANSWER 7.10

There are incestuous frame violations in the image of a brother- and sister-in-law being in bed together. This is the strongest frame-related image in the dream, which also has physical-setting frames—the bedroom and the school.

Incest looms large as a major theme in this dream. But lacking both guided associations to the surface dream and a trigger event that could give shape to the dream imagery, Jan's dream remains a puzzle. We are therefore compelled to move on and further develop the trigger decoding process so we finally can discover the secret message of Jan's dream. We'll do that in Chapter 8, but for now, let's turn to a final exercise in surface dream imagery.

EXERCISE

Recall a recent dream. Review the dream following the categories for the analysis of the face of a dream listed above. Explore the setting, the people, the action of the dream, and how things turn out. Use the surface dream to identify problems that are worrying you and see if there are clues as to how to handle them. Determine if the dream images lead you to concerns you hadn't realized you were worried about. Most important, reflect on the extent to which the surface dream is a working over of issues you're familiar with or in contrast, a reflection of issues you hadn't at all realized were on your mind.

In time, you can compare what you get from a surface dream with what you get from a dream-associational network as linked to its triggers. All too often, people use surface dreams to rehearse familiar problems instead of probing deeper to discover not only critical problems that had escaped their notice, but also the solutions to these elusive difficulties. This is why we will not take the surface dream too seriously.

SUMMING UP

The surface dream allows for a first and strictly limited foray into the world of dream experience. It is a bridge from conscious concerns to unconscious concerns, although by itself it belongs mostly to the world of conscious experience. It is often said that a dream is a reflection of the unconscious mind; however, this is not a true statement.

A *remembered* dream is a *conscious experience*. The dream is unusual because it typically takes the form of visual imagery and thinking and because it is initially experienced in the sleeping or altered state of consciousness. While this state of mind does indeed loosen our psychological defenses and allow for revelations that are unlikely in the waking state, by and large, the surface dream is part of our direct world of experience. If we keep that in mind, we're likely to want to get more from our dreams, as we can and should. For that reason among others, let's press forward.

Chapter 8

Guided Associations:
The Key to Thematic Power

We have entered this chapter with an incomplete exercise and a need to discover the trigger decoded meanings of
Jan's dream.

In engaging in this search, we are crossing an invisible
but vital line between the worlds of conscious and unconscious experience—the worlds of direct versus encoded
meaning.

To pursue the deeper strata, we need Jan's guided
associations to the main and most powerful elements of her
dream. The recall of a dream is the first step in its processing and engaging in storied associations called forth by the
details of the dream is the second. As I have indicated,
associating to a dream is an essential step in its processing
because every dream image is packed with a rather large
number of encoded stories that are condensed into its
imagery. And each of these stories will, as a rule, add to the
pool of strong themes which we need to develop for trigger
decoding the dream.

Before we establish some guidelines for how to do
guided associating, let's fill in a little more of Jan's dream-
associational network.

JAN'S GUIDED ASSOCIATIONS

Suppose that we now ask Jan to associate to the elements of her dream, to engage in guided associating. This is
what she would tell us: "Finding my husband in bed with
my sister brings to mind a movie about a homosexual man

who comes home one day to find his lover in bed with his best friend, another man. The man gets into a fight with his lover and stabs him with a knife, wounding him badly. Come to think of it," Jan adds, "Arthur is gay. He told me the other day of a friend of his who had died of AIDS; I felt very sad when I heard the story. Arthur says he's terrified of getting AIDS, but he is who he is, he can't change that."

At this point, Jan blanches. Suddenly, she remembers that her mother had called her earlier in the week to tell Jan that she had received a phone call from her brother, Alex, who is in the Middle East where he's a newsstation cameraman. It seems that her mother and brother began to quarrel—her mother couldn't recall why—and Alex had blurted out that he was gay and has been for years. He then tearfully told her that a man he loved, a reporter whom he had worked with, had been killed by a land mine.

Jan's mother was in shock and Jan had reacted to her mother's tale with a mixture of anxiety, anguish, concern, and sadness. She was worried that her brother might have or get AIDS or be killed while on assignment. She had cried for a long time after talking to her mother, but then she pulled herself together and decided there was nothing she could do but hope and pray her brother would be safe and well. She thought everything had been settled in her mind. Her dream-associational network seemed to be telling her otherwise.

QUESTION 8.1

Is this a series of *guided associations*—for example, do they take a dream image as their point of departure? And are these associations narrative or nonnarrative in nature?

ANSWER 8.1

These are indeed guided associations that begin with the dream imagery and wander away from there, though not too far away. And they are narrative in nature. A story from a movie leads to a story about Jan and her mother and brother.

> *Storied or narrative guided associations are ideal carriers of unconscious, encoded meaning.*

QUESTION 8.2

What are the strong themes in these associations? How do they compare in power to the themes in the surface dream from which they are drawn?

ANSWER 8.2

The strong themes are homosexuality, finding a lover with another man, betrayal, fighting, stabbing and wounding someone, illness and death due to AIDS, and being killed by a land mine. These are very strong themes and show considerably more power than the surface dream.

We can see again why dreams are dreamt to be associated to rather than analyzed and how guided associations enrich the thematic pool needed for linking themes to triggers. But there's more than fresh power in these guided associations, so let's press on.

QUESTION 8.3

Compare the surface dream with the guided associations. What themes do they share? What themes are introduced by the guided associations?

ANSWER 8.3

The main shared themes are those of inappropriate bed partners, betrayal, illness (being febrile and having AIDS), siblings, and sadness.

The new power themes are homosexuality, attacking/stabbing someone, death due to illness (AIDS), and violence (the land mine), loving a man and losing him (loss through death). The less strong new themes include a son upsetting his mother and sister, reporter and cameraman, dangerous assignment, telephone contact, and quarreling (between mother and son)—to name the most salient.

We see then that this single guided association has not only added an enormous amount of power to this narrative pool, but also a wide range of fresh thematic material.

> *Guided associations are the only way we can develop a full and telling pool of themes as we strive to reach into deep unconscious experience and wisdom via trigger decoding.*

THE SHIFT TO TRIGGERS

These guided associations also have presented us with a powerful trigger event for the dream. Let's pursue that trigger and shift for the moment from thematic development to trigger identification, the other half of the decoding process. We'll take that step here mainly so we can more fully develop our sense of how themes connect to triggers. We'll also see why themes need to be extracted from their surface contexts and related to the trigger events that have evoked them.

QUESTION 8.4

Identify the *trigger event* that has been revealed in these guided associations.

ANSWER 8.4

The trigger is the telephone call from her mother to Jan, which contained in it another trigger event of considerable emotional power, the things Alex had told their mother.

Jan's repression of that incident is, of course, surprising, but remarkably common.

> *We naturally obliterate and forget (repress) many major traumas and many aspects of the traumas we do recall.*

Once the telephone conversation was recalled, Jan remembered her *conscious* impressions and concerns, mainly, the possibility that her brother might die or be killed while on assignment. But in addition, you can be certain that there are disturbing implications to this trigger event that Jan had no awareness of at all because they were strongly repressed and perceived and processed unconsciously.

The purpose of processing and trigger decoding a dream is to get at these kinds of repressed impressions and perceptions so their effects can be held within bounds and dealt with.

Now that we have a strong trigger event, we can identify some of its meanings or attributes and see how Jan's mind disguised them to produce her encoded dream.

QUESTION 8.5

Identify the main themes of the stronger trigger event, the situation with Jan's brother. Is that trigger mentioned in the surface dream? If your answer is no—as it should be— this means that *aspects of the trigger event must be encoded in the surface dream in the form of bridging themes.* Note that at the moment we are discussing the dream as dreamt— the surface dream—and not the guided associations. Identify the main themes that bridge from the surface dream to the trigger event, the themes in the manifest dream that could be used to describe the evocative trigger.

ANSWER 8.5

In this case the trigger event's primary qualities are: homosexuality, concerns about illness and death due to AIDS or attack; its secondary qualities are the loss of a homosexual lover through death. These attributes are encoded in the surface dream as the discovery of an illicit heterosexual and incestuous affair between Jan's husband and her sister, and also via the them of illness.

To begin with the trigger, we see that through displacement and disguise the brother's homosexual affair is encoded as the sister's involvement with Jan's husband. The brother was transformed into the sister and the homosexual lover was transformed first into Jan's husband and then into Arthur. But through condensation, Arthur also encodes or represents Alex's homosexuality as well as the death of his lover and Jan's concern about her brother's health and safety.

It has been necessary to allude to themes in Jan's guided associations. To continue in this vein, the death of Arthur's friend also encodes the danger of death by other means such as through a land mine. Through condensation, the image of Arthur represents several different aspects of the trigger event and, in principle, several different triggers as well.

> *It is important for us to realize that neither the brother nor homosexuality—important power themes—can be found anywhere in the surface dream. It was only by invoking Jan' guided associations that these themes materialized, as did the trigger itself.*

You can see how tepid our previous yield was from working over the surface dream on its own compared to what we learned through this first guided association to the dream. And you can see how much more grim and anxiety-provoking the associated material was compared to the surface of the dream.

The deeper meanings of dreams relate not only to our psychological states, they profoundly influence how we behave, what we do, and the choices we make. On the day she spoke to her mother, Jan had impetuously fired a woman who worked for her. She had become convinced that the woman was a lesbian and was creating trouble in their office; however there was little evidence for these beliefs. You can see then that the subterranean issues we've been identifying in Jan's mind through processing her dream were exerting effects on Jan's life and actions of which she was quite unaware.

> *Important and powerful sources of her behaviors were entirely outside of her awareness; it seems likely she'd have thought and acted differently if she had processed her dream.*
>
> *It takes a lot for the conscious mind to be convinced that the world of surface and conscious experience is pale and unempowered compared to that of deep unconscious experience, but such is the case.*

Notice again that there is virtually no way that you could tell from the surface dream that Jan was working over the news that her brother was homosexual. It was so well disguised and encoded into this dream that only guided associating could bring it forth.

> *The ignorance we suffer without trigger decoding is enormous.*

Finally, it should be noted that we have not accounted for all of the power themes in this dream-associational network through our discussion of this one trigger. Therefore one more perspective should be added before we leave the dream behind us.

QUESTION 8.6

Further guided associations took Jan back to her childhood. Can you guess what early traumatic event was encoded in Jan's dream? Use the trigger and themes as your clues.

If you guessed that Alex had tried to seduce Jan, you are quite intuitive and adept at trigger decoding. If you missed that incident and guessed another trauma such as Jan finding her father in bed with another woman, your answer is also correct. If you guessed that Jan had found her mother in bed with another man or that she had found her sister in bed with Alex, you would have come up with answers that are quite viable in light of the surface dream imagery; the fact that they didn't happen is a moot point. Similarly, if you thought that somehow an illness in Jan's father or brother was also important, you would have made good use of the surface themes of the dream.

The key point for the moment is that themes are *evoked by* and *suggest* triggers and if you guessed a trigger that could have been represented by the themes of this dream, you have done very well.

As for Jan, it seems clear from her guided associations that she was having a strong adverse unconscious reaction, disguised in her dream, to learning about her brother's homosexuality. However, her dream-associational imagery alerted her to her conflicts in this area and to the need for additional dream decoding so she could get in touch with and resolve the underlying issues.

Unfortunately, Jan did not reap sufficient insight from the present dream-associational network to prevent her from precipitously firing the woman at work whom she imagined to be homosexual. Among the compelling reasons to engage in trigger decoding your dreams is the need to work over and resolve these kinds of anxieties and conflicts and their inadvertent displaced, misdirected, and misguided consequences.

But we're now a bit ahead of ourselves, so let's get back to guided associating and spell out the principles that pertain to carrying out this part of the dream process in the most productive manner possible.

GUIDED ASSOCIATING: HOW TO DO IT

Here are some leads on how to engage in guided associating:

1. Allow your mind to wander over the surface images in your dream with the goal of allowing the images to bring to mind one or more stories of some kind.
2. Once you think of a story, tell that story. Never pass over a narrative that occurs to you. If you do this, you can be certain that the defensive and avoidance needs of the conscious mind are at work.
3. Tell the story in as much detail as possible. The deep unconscious system likes to use the seemingly coincidental details of a central tale to convey much of what it wants to communicate.
4. If you think of a general period or time in your life, always pursue the image until a *specific* incident comes to mind. Thoughts of general events are weak carriers of encoded meaning. They serve mainly as markers of specific stories that need to be discovered and told.
5. When you think of a story, allow it to spin out as far as it goes. If a related story comes to mind, tell it. Keep going as long as narratives occur to you.
6. It is vital, however, to return to the dream elements for a fresh start before too long. Use your judgment and your sense of how strong

the themes in the extended story happen to be: strong themes are a signal to press on, while weak themes generally point to the need to go back to the surface dream for a fresh guided association.

7. Try to keep to storied guided associations because they carry the encoded themes you're trying to develop. If you slip into the nonstoried mode with some kind of intellectualization, recognize what you are doing. Go back to the dream elements to get a fresh association going. Departing from story telling is inevitable; the goal is to catch it as soon as possible and to shift back into the narrative mode.

8. Build your sequence of guided associations and the pool of themes they create without too much thought about the emerging themes and even less speculation as to what they might have to do with triggers. Mark strong themes for later work and allow your mind to automatically store the main themes in your stories, which will be ready for retrieval later on.

9. Keep in mind the necessity of generating several power themes through your stories. If power is lacking, keep associating until at least one story with strong themes comes to mind. Remember that you need power themes for meaningful linking to triggers and for a significant revelation and insight through processing your dream.

10. Finish up with most of your guided associating before turning to search for trigger events. Naive guided associations are optimal for processing a dream toward deep insight.

Remember a recent dream. Identify its strongest themes. Engage in guided associating to the dream elements. At first you should allow yourself to let your mind start with any dream image that you're drawn to and allow your thoughts to go where they will. Do not write down these associations, just keep them in mind. Once you've finished associating, answer the following questions:

QUESTION 8.7

- Did most or all of your associations take as their point of departure the specific elements of your dream?

- Did you see to it that you did not wander too far from the dream?

- Did you associate to all of the most powerful elements of the surface dream?

- How many of your associations were analytic and explanatory, like interpretations of the dream or an effort to say what the dream meant, in lieu of storied responses? Did you catch yourself when you slipped into intellectualizations and the nonstoried mode? Did you then generate a fresh storied guided association?

- Do you have some powerful new themes in your guided associations? By and large, do they exceed the surface dream in power?

- What new themes did your guided associations introduce into your pool of themes?

- If your feel adventuresome, try to find a currently active trigger for your pool of themes. Take the themes you have generated and connect them to the trigger, defining the themes as characterizing your unconscious perceptions of the trigger event.

- What new insight have you discovered in this way?

Begin this part of the process with your bridging imagery, the themes in your dream-associational network that tie in with and describe attributes of the trigger event you've chosen to work with. From there, use your power themes to characterize how you experienced your trigger event.

The answer to almost all of these questions should be in the affirmative and should speak for enriching and enlarging your pool of themes. If this is not the case, go back and try to rework your exercise until it is rich in thematic power and facilitates decoded insight.

It is helpful to practice associating to dream elements and to maintain a vigilance for intellectual, explanatory associations that take you away from the storied mode of expressing yourself. These nonstoried associations are inevitable because we all rotate in and out of storied and nonstoried communication and because the conscious mind is geared up for creating defensive obstacles to the eventual link between themes and triggers. Be on the alert for departures from the decoding process.

> *An essential responsibility in processing a dream is observing your own resistances or departures from the necessary steps needed to reach trigger decoded insights. It therefore is critical to learn the main components of this process and to keep them in mind as you try to process your dreams.*

The marvelous world of deep unconscious experience can be discovered and mastered through themes and triggers. We've spent this chapter developing themes, it's time now to turn to their triggers.

Chapter 9

Triggers:
What Dreams and Life are About

Life is about real events, it's not about dreams. Dreams in turn are not about our inner imaginations, they're about the surface and depth of life and what empowers our emotional problems and choices. The fact is, that dreams are active coping responses to life experiences. And they especially reflect the incredulous ways we cope unconsciously with emotional issues. The most valuable reward we can get from processing a dream is to unravel its encoded messages and access the profound encoded wisdom of our own minds.

Defensively, we tend to detach dreams from reality or to treat dreams as if dreamers stops coping with life's experiences when they are asleep. We think that dreams face inward rather than realizing that they first face outward and then inward. And even when we grant dreams a connection to reality, we either think of dreams as fantasies and day-dreams vaguely evoked by reality or we consider reality in broad strokes instead of specific incidents. We have developed countless ways to disconnect the dream from the most critical realities to which they are a response.

Dreams encode responses to emotionally vital triggers and to the implications of those trigger events that are most disturbing for us and to which we are most vulnerable. Dreams make sense only when decoded in light of their stimuli.

To illustrate this principle again, suppose you were watching a film of a man running down a street. You could say that the man was running but you'd be belaboring the obvious, as we often do with surface dreams. You'd know a lot more about his running as a coping or adaptive response if you knew what had set him off. Running would have one meaning if he were being chased by an assailant. But it would have a very different meaning if you learned that the woman the man loved was nearby and that he was running to meet her.

Notice that the same behavior has entirely different essential meanings depending on the stimulus or trigger for the behavior.

> *It is important to settle in your mind the realization that the same dream can have entirely different meanings depending on the trigger event to which it is a response.*

Let's experience this fact through an exercise.

EXERCISE

Belle dreams that she's trapped in a stuck elevator with a man with dark brown hair. She's very frightened that the elevator will fall to the ground and she'll be killed. The man takes her hands and reassures her everything will be alright. She then hears music being piped into the elevator through a speaker in the ceiling; the music is soothing and reassuring.

QUESTION 9.1

Can you think of one or more trigger events that might have prompted this dream and account for its themes? Try to think of something that could have happened to Belle to set off these personally chosen images and themes.

> *Remember that themes reflect triggers, and that the implications of a trigger event is captured in encoded form through the themes of a dream and its guided associations.*

We are looking to develop the ability to match themes to triggers which is an indispensable aspect of trigger decoding.

If you named an entrapping trigger of any kind you are on the right track. Entrapment comes up whenever we secure a frame or obey a ground rule, such as when we commit to a relationship or a situation of any kind. Entrapment also comes up when someone invades our space or in some way has control over our lives. It also arises from traumas in enclosed spaces like a car accident and from experiences in which we feel helpless like a serious illness, injury, and death.

Before we get to the actual trigger for this dream, let's try out a few triggers to see how each of them shapes these themes in their own way, thereby producing a *distinctive* unconscious message.

One possible trigger event could be that one of Belle's boyfriends had died of AIDS. The dream then reflects Belles' anxiety that she too has contracted the disease and will die. She is trying to reassure herself that this will not happen. The elevator represents the coffin and death, while the music represents the funeral music played at the boyfriend's funeral.

Another possible trigger for this same dream could be that Belles' father is ill and she's trapped in the city where he lives and can't leave. She feels she'll suffer terribly if she doesn't leave, but the dream is pointing her to ways she can survive in the city, an adaptive solution. The music alludes to her talents as a musician (she's an excellent pianist) and the theme is shaped to suggest that making better use of these talents could solve her problem for a while.

You can see that the same image has very different meanings depending on the trigger event. To illustrate this further, let's look again at the allusion to the music. With the first trigger, it is a funeral dirge, while with the second trigger, it is a sign of creativity and of hope for a better life.

> *Every dream and every dream image is specifically honed as a particular encoded response to a particular trigger event. On the level of its most compelling meanings and utility, there's no such thing as a dream symbol or a universal dream, no possible single meaning to a given dream or dream image— only a specific, personal meaning in light of who you are and the nature of the specific trigger to which your dream is an encoded coping response.*

This is why only you and you alone can process your dreams, only you can associate meaningfully to them, and only you can find their most compelling triggers. This is why dreams are dreamt to be associated to, so you can build a network of themes to enable you to enter the world of unconscious experience in light of your emotional issues and their trigger events. None of this can be done through dream symbols or by extracting meaning from the surface of a dream and your guided associations to it without knowing its trigger.

With this in mind, let's turn to how you can learn to discover your most powerful triggers, the great provocateurs for your dream experiences.

THE SEARCH FOR TRIGGERS

On the face of it, we tend to believe that we know what upsets us emotionally. But careful studies of the emotion-processing mind reveals that the human mind has been designed by evolution to keep knowledge of that kind to an utter minimum—to have us know as little as possible consciously about our emotionally charged issues and triggers. Many of the incidents we do remember are quickly forgotten or put aside, while those we don't forget are reduced to a few cold facts, and the nuances and emotional impact tend to be forgotten, if they were noticed in the first place. Most important, these events are almost never connected to a set of encoded themes, which means that the unconscious experience of the trigger event cannot be marked out, decoded, and comprehended.

Trigger events are, by and large, critical but elusive moments in our lives.

It takes *work* and *concentration* to bring triggers into focus, to appreciate their strongest implications, and to then link a discovered trigger to a dream-associational network in a way that reveals your actual unconscious experience of that trigger event.

QUESTION 9.2

Generating guided associations tends to become rather easy with practice. All you need to do is keep the search for storied associations in mind and keep pressing for more and more narrative material. In time, you're likely to have the ability to generate powerful networks of themes.

But given that triggers slip through our fingers so easily, what can you do to insure that to the greatest extent possible, you've found your most important triggers? Think through this question as best you can and record your answer.

The question is best answered with a few guidelines:

1. In searching for triggers, try first to list all of the most emotionally charged experiences of the dream day that you can remember. To assist you with this direct listing effort, I will soon discuss the kinds of triggers that are most likely to set off strong unconscious reactions as revealed in dreams. This method of drawing directly on your memory for the identification of emotionally charged trigger events from the day or two before a dream (with very powerful triggers the duration of unconscious responsiveness is somewhat longer) is called the *trigger listing method of trigger recognition.*

2. Try out these directly recalled triggers with your themes. If you get a thematic fit—if the themes go well with the implications of the trigger event—work out what it all means. If nothing seems to gel, then look for more triggers.

3. After identifying every recent trigger you can remember directly, turn to your themes.

   Think of your themes in your dream-associational network as encoded descriptions of your triggers, and allow them to suggest triggers to you.

   Using the themes in a surface dream and its guided associations to direct you to important trigger events is called *the themes to trigger method of trigger discovery.*

4. While anything with an emotional aspect can be a trigger event, there is a special class of triggers to which we're very sensitive uncon-

sciously: frames such as ground rules and laws. Get acquainted with these kinds of impingements or stimulus events and keep them in mind as you move across your themes, allowing them to suggest triggers to you. Most significant traumas involve some kind of rule-breaking, violation of the law, encroachment of personal boundaries, and violations of secured frames and contexts.

5. If you identify a repressed or missed trigger event through your themes, take your entire pool of themes and connect it to the trigger event in order to get a full sense of your unconscious experience of that trigger.

6. A strong surface dream and/or strong guided associations indicate a strong trigger experience; search until you find the right trigger for that kind of dream-associational network.

Life has two kinds of days. The first is a seemingly routine day with many lesser emotional experiences. But some of these events affect our unconscious minds rather strongly through their consciously unnoticed traumatic implications, even though their surface happenings are not especially dramatic.

The second kind of day is that in which something powerful and clearly hurtful emotionally occurs. The trauma can range from a marvelous success or moment of intense satisfaction to the loss of a loved one, an accident, an assault, illness, or loss of a job.

In the first situation, your personal sensitivities and abilities for identifying your triggers will serve you well. In time, you can get to know the kind of hurts and satisfactions that cause you trouble. In doing so, you must realize that *conscious* sensitivities often are different from *unconscious* sensitivities. Get to know your own world of unconscious experience; it will greatly clarify and enhance your life.

In the second situation, there's a conscious tendency to want to block out your unconscious experience of the trauma. After a severely hurtful experience, the conscious mind automatically goes into a defensive mode. With a trauma like a fatal accident or the death of a loved one, it is not uncommon at first to not remember your dreams at all—messages from the deep unconscious system are obliterated. But over the ensuing days, dreams begin to stick with you and become available for processing. It then becomes possible through guided associating and linking themes to triggers to work over the powerful unconscious effects the traumatic experience has had on you.

EXERCISE

Beth is a young woman who works as a computer consultant for a large firm. At the time of the Christmas holidays she awakes one morning to find her husband, Al, in an irritable mood. They exchange words and she goes to work.

At her office, Beth discovers that her secretary has made a serious error regarding an estimate for services Beth was submitting to a major client. Soon after, she chats with two of the men in her company, one of whom is critical of a recent job Beth had completed.

Beth then goes off to work with a major client on a new computer system they're installing. At her client's office, the head of the company sits her down and asks a number of pressing questions about how Beth is proceeding. He tells her that his friend, who's the head of another corporation, had to scuttle his entire computer system because the glitches couldn't be straightened out. He doesn't want that to happen with this installation. He can remember when his father ran the corporation with just five employees; if someone didn't do things right, they were gone before they knew what had hit them.

The rest of the afternoon is spent working on the new computer programs and interacting with various employees of the company for which Beth was doing the work. That evening there is an office Christmas party that Beth and her husband both attend. At the party, her boss dances with her twice and presses her closer to himself than Beth is comfortable with. She notices that his wife is not at the party and wonders what that means.

During the ride home with Al they talk, again, about having a baby. Al speaks of wanting to be a father even though most of what he says has to do with the ways in which having a baby would cut down on their freedom to do things, increase their responsibilities, add to their financial burdens, and change their lives for the worse. Beth speaks mainly about being tired of working and wanting a child and a family. When they get home, Al wants to have intercourse with Beth, who reluctantly agrees but feels detached from the experience, especially since Al insists on wearing a condom.

When Beth awakes the next morning, she remembers a dream. In the dream she is trying to make her bed but a man keeps messing it up. Half playfully, she throws a pillow at him and he comes over and slams her against a wall.

QUESTION 9.3

This small sample of one day in Beth's life has a number of trigger events in both her job situation and in her relationship with her husband. Name as many of Beth's triggers as you can. Try to begin your answer with the most powerful trigger you can identify and list the rest of the triggers in the decreasing order of their evident strength.

ANSWER 9.3

The most powerful series of trigger events appears to be Beth's discussion with her husband about having a baby and, specifically, his negative comments about the subject and his asking to have intercourse with her and then using a condom. Perhaps the next strongest trigger is Beth's boss' dancing closely with her and seeming to be behaving seductively. Other lesser but emotionally important triggers include the error made by Beth's secretary which was creating a lot of grief for Beth, the critical comments made to Beth by a fellow worker, and the veiled threat made by Beth's client to the effect that if the job she was doing didn't go well, she'd be dropped.

This is a small sampling of triggers in the day of the life of an average working woman. It should give you a sense of just how complicated we've made our lives these days. For most of us, emotionally charged triggers accumulate with remarkable rapidity. It would be impossible to pause and consciously work over the aroused emotional issues each time we were slighted, hurt, seduced, attacked, and otherwise traumatized and bruised psychologically or even physically; we'd have no time for anything else and we'd soon perish.

Small wonder that natural selection favored minds that developed the capacity to perceive and process emotional traumas and hurts outside of awareness. The miracle is that this unconscious processing involves a powerful adaptive intelligence that we build within ourselves through unconscious developmental experiences from infancy on. We are at our best in the emotional realm when we function without awareness.

It certainly is adaptive to put aside all but the most overwhelming traumas we suffer each day. But it also would be adaptive to be able to work over these traumas unconsciously and to then have the means of bringing this processing effort into awareness so we can benefit from our unconscious wisdom. But that's where a key problem arises.

> *The perceptions and issues at stake are so painful and infuriating and discombobulating to behold, that the human mind is designed so that none of this working over is accessible to awareness. However, necessity compels us to gain access to these images through trigger decoding because they powerfully determine most of our emotional reactions, choices, conflicts, and successes.*

To get a picture of how our minds unconsciously have been coping with these problems, we need to go against our natural alignment of defenses by using all of the available thematic imagery and the process of *trigger decoding*.

> *Given that our minds are designed to keep repressed and hidden many of our most powerful emotional experiences, we must carefully and insistently carry out each step in processing a dream so we can discover its secret triggers and unravel the best solutions to the dilemmas they pose. Persistence and vigilance are essential.*

Question 9.4

Examine Beth's surface dream. What is its most powerful theme? Overall, how powerful is the dream? And what do its themes tell you?

Answer 9.4

As discussed earlier, we begin our dream processing effort by looking quickly at the surface dream. In this case, the dream is rather brief and shows only a small amount of power. That power is reflected in the man's slamming Beth against a wall—a hurtful power theme. The rest of the dream is rather innocuous—there's a sense of conflict, but not of power.

The face of this dream suggests that Beth sees men as interfering with her goals and what she wants to do. It also speaks for her having a playful attitude toward men, but this is countered by a hostile, violent response by the man.

Again we find that in looking at a surface dream in isolation, we can't tell if these are inner conflicts within Beth or reflections of actual hurts she has experienced from men and perhaps women as well.

Question 9.5

If you confine yourself to the triggers we have just identified, can you connect the themes of this dream with any of those triggers? What do the themes of Beth's surface dream tell you about those trigger events?

ANSWER 9.5

The clearest connection between the themes of Beth's surface dream—mainly the assault—and the triggers she suffered seems to be with the criticism her fellow worker had made and with the threat made by Beth's client. In each case, Beth had felt threatened and attacked psychologically by the remarks they had made. In light of each of these trigger events, her dream indicates that Beth had experienced their comments as unexpectedly attacking. However, this insight adds only minimally to what Beth already was aware of.

We also can connect these dream images to Beth's discussion with her husband of getting pregnant. While Al did not attack Beth, consciously she felt put off and annoyed by his attitude. However, her surface dream indicates that with Al too Beth felt assaulted despite his good intentions. It is possible that Al's pressures on Beth to have intercourse with him also was experienced in this way.

With these trigger situations, the dream adds a bit more to Beth's understanding; she hadn't realized consciously how much she had felt attacked by her husband. This connection between that particular group of triggers and the dream themes also explains why Beth woke up the next morning extremely annoyed with her husband without knowing why. Unwittingly, she gave him a hard time with everything he did before he left the apartment for work. Deep unconscious influence was having its effects on Beth's feelings and actions.

Connecting the surface dream themes with these trigger events begins to shape our understanding of the dream and indicates some of the ways Beth was unconsciously processing her trigger experiences. But clearly the yield is thin; we need something more.

What more do we in fact need?

We need Beth's guided associations so we have more themes and especially some additional power themes to link to her triggers.

Asked to associate to her dream, Beth says that making the bed brings to mind a film story about a woman who had been date raped in her own bedroom, on her bed, and had become pregnant and then had an abortion. Being slammed into the wall reminded Beth of an incident when she was in her teens and her brother came into her bedroom and started to get physical and sexual with her. When he wouldn't stop, she got up and slammed him against the wall. He hit his head and was groggy for a while, but he never got fresh with her again.

These are Beth's guided associations. We want to bring them into the processing of the dream. How powerful are these fresh stories? How do they compare in power with Beth's surface dream? Extract the main themes from these new stories and state the nature of the strongest themes.

ANSWER 9.7

Clearly, the power of Beth's guided associations—and it is considerable—far exceeds that of her surface dream. The main themes are rape, abortion, incestuous seduction, defensive assault, and injury via concussion. In stating these themes as such, freed from their surface stories or contexts, we have a set of powerful themes that can be brought into linkage with Beth's trigger events and read out as her unconscious experience of those events, and her reactions to her experience as well.

QUESTION 9.8

Which triggers do these new themes best link up with? Take the strongest trigger and make up a story that tells how Beth has unconsciously perceived the trigger event and how she reacted to what she experienced.

ANSWER 9.8

The themes of intercourse, impregnation, and abortion seem most closely connected to the issue of Beth becoming pregnant. Unconsciously, Beth had experienced her husband's remarks as assaultive and the intercourse they had engaged in as rapacious and incestuous. Beth's guided associations also indicate that the surface dream image of her being thrown against a wall encodes both Beth's feeling of assault at the hands of her husband and her own reactive anger at his recalcitrance about having a baby. Here, *condensation* operates in a way that allows the surface dream image of the harmful man to represent both Beth and her husband and, in addition, Beth's secretary and the several men who had threatened Beth that day.

We see again the interplay between themes and triggers. As for triggers, we learn the following:

1. Once you've developed your dream and guided associations, *make up a trigger list of your main active triggers*, especially those from the day of the dream and strong residual triggers that you are likely to still be working over.

2. *List the most powerful triggers first* and then concentrate on these triggers, allowing the lesser triggers to stay in the back of your mind. If time permits, you can also process these less strong triggers in terms of your themes.

3. *Connect the most powerful triggers to your most powerful themes.* Always read out the themes as your unconscious experience of the trigger event—as unconscious perceptions and the working over of these impressions—and not as some kind of inner fantasy or wish.

4. Once your unconscious experience has been defined, *read out the remaining themes as your reaction to your perceptions of the trigger event.*

5. Go through your themes to see if they bring to mind repressed or unnoticed trigger events. *In every effort to process a dream, there will be repressed or missed triggers.* This occurs partly because each day there simply are too many emotionally relevant triggers for us to recognize and work over consciously, which is also why we process many of them outside of

awareness where far more information and meaning can be dealt with than is possible consciously. Repressed triggers also are common because their implications are too painful and disturbing for us to allow them into awareness.

6. Every effort to process a dream, which ultimately involves processing the most critical triggers of a dream day, should include an active search for repressed triggers. *Unaccounted for, powerful themes in the dream-associational network are the best clues to these missing triggers.*

FINDING A REPRESSED OR MISSING TRIGGER EVENT

This brings us to a final addendum to Beth's dream processing efforts. In searching for missing triggers, Beth went over her strongest themes several times. She kept coming back to the incident with her brother. Why was she experiencing her husband as an incestuous brother; it didn't quite make sense.

As she reflected on this uncertainty, Beth suddenly remembered that her brother had called her at her office on the day of the dream. She was surprised she had forgotten the call, especially since her brother had called to tell Beth he was getting divorced for the second time.

Beth's brother had sounded strange on the telephone. He spoke of coming to live with Beth, of his sexual problems with his wife, and of how much sex he needs to keep himself content.

This repressed trigger helped even more to convincingly explain the appearance of her memory about her brother in her guided associations. And this particular trigger, which Beth had dismissed as her brother having his troubles again, links well to the other themes in Beth's dream-associational network; the call had been unconsciously experienced as inappropriately invasive, seductive, and attacking.

The networks we weave in the incredibly complex world of human emotions seem to defy conscious imagination. And the defenses we automatically invoke are, at times, astounding. We therefore should not be surprised that even when her brother appeared in her associations to her dream, Beth still didn't remember that he had called her that day. Emotionally the human mind is extremely defensive in design, as you will discover personally when you begin to process your own dreams and triggers.

EXERCISE

Try to remember the dream you had last night. If all of your dreams are lost, make up a short story. Engage in guided associating to the dream elements.

QUESTION 9.9

Starting with those that are strongest, list the main themes in your dream and in your guided associations. And once again, compare the power of the two lists of themes.

ANSWER 9.9

The power of the themes in your guided associations should, as a rule, be greater than that of the themes in your surface dream. If this is not the case, you should press on for more associated stories; powerful themes are there somewhere.

Every viable dream-associational network should have a measure of power—the unconscious mind is always dealing with unnoticed but compelling emotional concerns.

QUESTION 9.10

List all of the trigger events of note from the day of your dream. Order the list so the most powerful triggers come first. As you think through your day, you're likely to find that your list gets longer and longer; trigger events are legion.

ANSWER 9.10

With concentration, you should have a lengthy list of emotionally strong trigger events. Just about everything of importance in your life, no matter what the arena, has an emotional component. It is well to learn to quickly identify your most compelling, *active* triggers, and to then select for processing those that are most vital to your needs and concerns. This selection process should be directed by the themes in your narrative pool because the deep unconscious system which has produced those themes knows full well which triggers are having the greatest impact on your psyche. As a result, your *strongest themes* will tend to organize around your *strongest triggers*.

Go over your themes with the idea of allowing them to suggest a trigger or two that you've repressed and missed until now.

With a mixture of openness and concentration, you should be able to come up with one or more repressed or forgotten triggers. Not infrequently, you will come upon a major traumatic trigger you had put out of your mind. Don't be surprised when this happens; it's all in the design of the mind.

Once we have a sense of the role that trigger events play in our lives, we can appreciate that *dream processing* and *decoding* is really *trigger processing* and *decoding*—dreams are a way of working over their triggers. Trigger processing requires trigger identification and a pool of themes that will reveal the dreamer's unconscious experience of the trigger events.

With themes and triggers in hand, all that needs to be done is to link one to the other. With this one last effort, the world of unconscious experience will stand revealed to the conscious mind. Let's see now just how this final step in dream processing is carried out.

Chapter 10

Insight:
Linking Themes to Their Triggers

When it comes to the world of unconscious experience and to processing a dream vis-a-vis our trigger experiences, there is only one definition of insight and understanding— the moment when themes are linked to their triggers.

There are many kinds of formulations that are offered as deep understanding, but almost all of them are related to the world of conscious rather than unconscious experience. Of course, conscious experience often needs illumination. But as it has been pointed out, these deeper truths and insights that have far more power over our lives than do most conscious realizations. And these deeper truths about ourselves and others become available as a resource only when we connect our themes to our triggers and state the connection as a decoded unconscious perception of the trigger events and their implications.

True and crucial deep meaning is arrived at in processing a dream only when strong themes are linked to strong triggers.

In working with dreams, too many trivial and irrelevant pronouncements are called insight. These *pseudo*insights actually deceive us into believing we've arrived at a notable punch line, but they seldom change a life or enforce deeply adaptive solutions to our emotional dilemmas. By and large, they are highly defensive ways of leading a person to believe that they have accomplished something in working with a dream when the main achievement has really been finding a way to avoid the most compelling and important meanings of the dream and its triggers.

To safeguard the processing of a dream and to insure that genuine deep insight has been arrived at, you must keep to the definition of meaning that states that *deep insight exists only when themes are linked to their triggers*. This is how the power of emotional life is revealed and this is how you can be master over that power instead of its slave— *linking* is the key to it all.

THE LINKING PROCESS

Linking is the moment of synthesis, of insight, of understanding your key triggers and how they've affected you unconsciously. It is the moment you access the solutions your own mind has unconsciously developed to solve your emotional problems.

QUESTION 10.1

Review the steps that lead to linking. Define linking and indicate the form it should take.

ANSWER 10.1

The steps to linking are the steps through which a dream is processed so your triggers can be understood in depth. They are:

1. Remember the dream.
2. Generate guided associations evoked by the elements and images of the dream.
3. Collect the themes in the surface dream and guided associations into a pool of themes.
4. Extract these themes by lifting them from the stories in which they are embedded and allowing them to float loosely in your mind, awaiting the triggers to which they will be connected.
5. Identify the most pertinent of your current triggers (processing must always begin with currently active triggers and fan out from there into the past and future).
6. Select the most compelling trigger events for linking up with the pool of themes.
7. Work with one trigger at a time, connecting the implications of the trigger event to the meanings of the themes.
8. State this linkage in terms of actual unconscious experience and then add your reaction to that experience.
9. Once you've made your decoded statement as a narrative explanation, you should go back to the original surface dream and develop one or more fresh guided associations.
10. These associations should be assessed to determine if they *confirm* or *fail to confirm* your proposed trigger decoded insight.
11. Confirmatory or nonconfirmatory stories are those that *follow a trigger decoded formulation or interpretation.* They are not part of the original dream-associational network, but are embodied in the specific storied responses to an effort to link themes to triggers in order to

define deep unconscious experience and its implications. The narratives conjured up after this attempt at linking speak to the value and validity of these efforts at understanding.

Follow-up stories with positive images and themes about wise and well functioning people speak for a valid decoded statement, while negative images of error, ignorance, blindness, and poor functioning speak for an incorrect formulation and to the need for reformulation.

In carrying out this process we use and shape only the available themes and triggers. We do not introduce extraneous material or ideas. Let's engage now in a series of exercises in linking themes to triggers.

EXERCISE

Dan dreams that he is skiing and takes a bad fall but he's only bruised.

In associating to the dream, the skiing reminds Dan of a ski weekend he took with a past girlfriend, Nan. The trip ended badly when Nan secretly got involved with another man and broke up with Dan. The ski accident reminds him of a friend who was killed in a skiing accident when he was hit from behind by an out-of-control skier, a woman who was just learning how to ski. The dead friend was a car salesman who was afraid to drive a car because he had had a premonition that he'd be maimed in a car accident. All his life he'd been convinced that he could foretell how he would die.

QUESTION 10.2

To begin as always with basics, is this dream and its guided associations storied or nonstoried in nature?

Answer 10.2

Both the surface dream and the associations are narrative tales. The material speaks for encoded communication and lends itself to processing toward deep insight.

Question 10.3

In terms of power, compare the themes in the surface dream with those in the guided associations.

Answer 10.3

Once again, the themes in the guided associations are far more powerful than those in the surface dream. They also are more varied and therefore help to create a stronger and richer pool of themes than the one we had with the dream alone. Here too, the surface dream has only minimal meaning; it is about a slight injury. And, again, the guided associations take the dream into cogent areas far beyond its surface images.

Question 10.4

Name the most compelling themes introduced into the pool of themes by the guided associations. Which themes appear to be most powerful?

Answer 10.4

The main themes that were added to the pool of themes through the guided associations are, in the sequence that they were introduced, those of betrayal, having an illicit affair, accidents and being accidentally killed, indications of a phobic fear (driving a car), and the unrealistic belief that one can foretell the future and how one will die. While these are all *power themes*, the most powerful among them seems to be those of death, an illicit affair, and the (unrealistic) ability to see the future.

Question 10.5

Lift the main themes out of the dream and associations to make them available for linking to their evocative triggers. Hold these extracted themes in mind, awaiting a trigger event to which you will be able to connect them.

Now, offer your speculations as to the kind of trigger events that could have evoked and given meaning to these images. Remember to look for clues in possible bridging imagery or themes that could move from the encoded dream and associations to the trigger event. The question, then, is can you identify some trigger events or incidents that could connect to these themes which are captured by the threads in this pool of themes?

Answer 10.5

To answer this question we must take the themes in the narrative pool and treat them as *bridging themes*. There are, of course, many possible emotionally charged events that could have evoked these themes. Some of the possibilities that arise in connection with the surface dream itself include a hurtful incident while skiing or in any other sport or setting, and/or an injury or illness suffered by Dan or someone close to him.

The guided associations present us with many more possibilities. There could have been any number of ways in which Dan has been hurt or jilted recently by a woman or he himself could be involved in some kind of sexual betrayal of his present girlfriend (Dan was single).

> *Keep in mind that we are looking for a currently active trigger event. In the world of dreams and unconscious experience, the past arises only in light of the present.*

Other possibilities include someone recently dying or having had an accident or any kind of trauma in which Dan's expectations were thwarted. To these we can add any number of trigger events that involve hurts from women and a wide range of possible accidents, illnesses, or death.

The actual trigger for this dream-associational network eluded Dan at first. But with the help of his themes he realized that, unconsciously, he was working over the unexpected death of Corine, a coworker, who was killed in an automobile accident. Her car had been hit from behind by a student driver and pushed in front of oncoming traffic, causing a head-on collision with another vehicle.

Corine's death was being worked over unconsciously and the processing was revealed in the images and themes in Dan's pool of themes. While the bridging theme of accidental death is quite apparent, there is a repressed aspect of this trigger event that is encoded in Dan's images and even less available to his awareness than the momentarily forgotten or repressed fact that his coworker had been killed.

The unconsciously perceived and experienced part of this trauma involved Dan's perceptions of Corine's attraction to him and his responsive attraction to her. Corine was married, so the attraction was unconsciously experienced as illicit.

As Dan began to understand his imagery in relation to their triggers, he realized that he felt some guilt over Corine's accidental death and that he had been ready to betray his present girlfriend by becoming involved with Corine, an intention that was unconsciously viewed as one that eventually would lead to damage and disaster—via condensation, the skiing accident encodes Corine's accident and Dan's unconscious perceptions of the consequences of his involvement with Corine.

At this juncture, Dan came up with another association to his dream, one evoked by the image of skiing. It suddenly occurred to him that it was at a softball game (a sporting event) that the mutual attraction between Corine and himself had become apparent. This further *bridging image* seemed to bring the entire network together and made it clear to Dan that he had a lot more processing to do in connection with Corine's death.

QUESTION 10.6

Try now to link the themes in this pool of themes to its evocative trigger event.

Use the themes to generate a statement of cause and effect.

The statement should take the general form of saying that the trigger event had evoked this or that experience in Dan and that he had reacted to the experience in this or that way.

ANSWER 10.6

With Dan telling the story, the themes would connect to this trigger event in the following way: "I realize that you were killed in a car accident with a student driver and I've reacted to that reality by wishing the injury was less than fatal, just a mere bruise. I also wish you had been able to foretell the accident or that you hadn't driven your car.

"Your death also has brought up my unconscious perceptions of your attraction to me and mine to you. The helplessness I feel in response to your unexpected loss is so great I want to believe that I am omniscient, that I can foretell the future. I am remembering that time at the softball game when you sort of came on to me. I hadn't realized until now how much you were attracted to me—and I to you. I realize too that I wanted to have an affair with you, to betray my girlfriend, and that the affair would have been illicit and hurtful to ourselves and others, a fatal attraction."

This is a sample of a *trigger decoded insight*. Dan accidentally had cut himself on a jagged piece of metal. It seems likely that this self-hurtful act was his own punishment for his activated wishes toward Corine. By bringing his conflicted feelings and perceptions of Corine into awareness, Dan could work them over without future self-harm.

Having offered this trigger decoded interpretation to Dan, we should now ask him to generate a fresh guided association to his surface dream.

He responds that the ski slopes bring to mind another time he had gone skiing and met this very attractive woman. She was not only beautiful, she also was very perceptive and smart. She was French and he was American, so nothing came of their affair. Nevertheless, it was one of the most satisfying relationships he had had in years.

QUESTION 10.7

Do these fresh guided associations strike you as confirming the formulation we made to Dan of his material or do you see them as nonconfirmatory?

ANSWER 10.7

Images of bright and attractive, well functioning people speak for the accuracy and positive value of the formulation we offered to Dan. His fresh storied guided association can be taken to validate much of what we proposed.

TWO TYPES OF DREAM/TRIGGER PROCESSING

There are two ways in which dream processing unfolds.

The first is the kind we just studied. The processing begins with the build up of a pool of themes via the remembered dream and guided associations. The themes then await the discovery of the critical triggers for the thematic material. Once a significant trigger is discovered, linking can be done and deep insight achieved.

The second sequence begins with an identified, known traumatic trigger event. The dreamer is well aware that someone is ill or has died, that they have just lost their job, that someone has hurt or abandoned them, and so on. With the trigger in hand, all that is needed is a pool of themes, and it is developed by turning to a recent dream and invoking guided associations.

It is important with this sequence of *trigger first* and *themes second* to let the trigger event recede to the back of your mind and to allow the recall of the dream and the invocation of guided associations to be as naive and unbiased as possible. You can rely on the deep unconscious system to generate the themes you need to understand your triggers. Just give that system the freedom to do so via naive story telling using dreams to evoke guided associations.

EXERCISE

Carla is a middle-aged, divorced woman who has just been told that she has breast cancer. Her doctor assures her that the lesion is localized and that there are no signs of it having spread. He advises her that with surgery alone her chances of recovery are good.

That night she dreams her friend Marge is sitting with her on her living room couch. They hear a noise in the hallway and some kind of disfigured monster with a red face comes into the living room. Carla awakes in terror as the monster is coming to strangle her.

QUESTION 10.8

How powerful are the themes in Carla's surface dream? Identify the main power themes.

Answer 10.8

This surface dream has a single measure of power in the image of the monster who is about to attack Carla. The themes are those of assault and of an event that could not happen in reality—there no monsters.

Question 10.9

What is the trigger for this dream?

Answer 10.9

While there must be additional triggers for this dream, the main identified trigger is having a lump in her breast and, especially, the diagnosis of cancer made by Carla's doctor.

Question 10.10

Even without guided associations, can you link these extracted themes to the implications of Carla's trigger event?

Answer 10.10

Carla appears to be experiencing her cancer as an assaultive monster who wants to harm or destroy her. Evidently, she is seeking the companionship or support of a friend as well.

Once more the yield from a surface dream alone is quite thin and closely linked to the dreamer's conscious experience and feelings. Let's therefore press on for some guided associations to this dream. This is what came to Carla's mind.

Carla remembers that Marge had had ovarian cancer. Pressing herself for a specific story, she recalls that Marge had been suffering from abdominal pain for about two years before a diagnosis was made. Her doctors thought she had gall bladder disease and then colitis and then a chronic appendicitis. It was only when they decided finally to remove her appendix that the tumor, which, fortunately, was small, was found. For a long time, Marge was in a rage against her doctors and she sued one of them for malpractice, which was still pending.

QUESTION 10.11

What are the main power themes in this guided association?

ANSWER 10.11

The main power themes are cancer, misdiagnosis, surgery, and suing for malpractice.

QUESTION 10.12

Extract these themes, lift them from the surface story about Marge, and place them into Carla's trigger situation. What is the main bridging theme? What unmentioned trigger could account for these fresh themes? Can you detect an aspect of the overall trigger event, the diagnosis of Carla's breast cancer, that she has not as yet alluded to?

The bridging theme is cancer—in Marge and in Carla's trigger—indicating that the story about Marge must be connected to Carla's trigger event.

The question now is this: what does this fresh story add to the picture of Carla's experience of this diagnosis. The new themes that now must be linked to that trigger situation are those of misdiagnosis, corrective surgery, anger, and suing for malpractice.

Carla expects to be operated on, so there's nothing unconscious about that theme. But what about the theme of missed diagnosis? Actually, therein lies a story which, at the moment, Carla is unaware of.

Consciously, Carla had accepted the diagnosis of breast cancer with resignation and deep dread. As she thought over the situation, however, she decided that she was irritated by the way her gynecologist had talked to her about the lesion after it was confirmed with mammography. She didn't like her attitude and was going to change doctors.

Beneath this consciously rationalized decision lay Carla's *unconscious perception* that her doctor had missed the tumor during an examination of Carla's breast only six months earlier. Without awareness, Carla also was wondering why her doctor had not sent her for annual mammograms. Unconsciously, then, Carla perceived her physician as having missed her diagnosis and the decision to change doctors was based as much on that unconscious perception as it was on any conscious feeling about how the doctor addressed Carla. While Carla was consciously irritated with her physician, unconsciously she was in a rage and wanted to sue her doctor for malpractice.

Carla was unaware of this fury and she displaced it onto several of her friends and especially her mother, from whom she decided to conceal her problem, a decision that, once revealed, would most certainly upset her mother and make Carla feel guilty for having not told her. Still, without trigger decoding her reaction this traumatic trigger event, many of the aspects of the situation are repressed and never reach awareness. It is these unconscious impressions and experiences that wreak havoc with one's emotional life unless they are commandeered through trigger decoding.

> *Every major trauma has disturbing aspects and implications that are repressed and never reach awareness. They are perceived and processed outside of awareness and can be realized and understood only through careful trigger decoding. Failing that, these unconscious images and their meanings operate through displacement onto other situations and relationships and can greatly upset a person's emotional life.*

In this situation, the trigger event was known, so the linking process required a pool of themes for it to go forward. As expected, the thematic imagery centered around repressed aspects of the trigger situation. The linking process allowed for the trigger decoding of the unconsciously perceived part of the experience of which Carla was unaware.

QUESTION 10.13

Take Carla's guided association and link it to the trigger event. Shape your statement in cause and effect terms. The model formulation is: this is what was experienced unconsciously about the trigger event and this is how the dreamer reacted to what she experienced.

Linking these fresh themes to the trigger event, Carla is saying that the doctor missed her diagnosis, and that Carla is in a rage over it and thinking of suing her for malpractice. "You [her doctor] failed me and I am furious and want to sue you." That is the essence of the decoded story.

Notice that once more the surface dream holds no clue to this repressed impression and Carla's reaction to it. In the surface dream, Marge appears as a friend and nothing more. It is only through Carla's guided association that we discover one of several stories condensed into the simple appearance of Marge in Carla's dream.

For example, Marge also represented Carla's grandmother who had had breast cancer many years earlier and who was another person whom Carla unconsciously blamed for her illness; but, at the moment, consciously she had forgotten this fact. Yet that particular unconscious story was another unconscious reason that Carla was so provocative with her mother at this time. Undecoded unconscious perceptions and memories of this kind derail our emotional lives unless we bring them to light through linking and trigger decoding.

THE QUESTION OF CONFIRMING A FORMULATION

Having offered Carla our decoded formulation of her encoded story, we are obliged to ask her to go back to her dream and offer us a new guided association. She responds by thinking of another story about Marge.

Carla and Marge had gone to Europe on vacation. Carla had become ill with what seemed like a gastrointestinal virus. They were in Italy at the time and neither of them spoke Italian. Nonetheless, Marge somehow was able to speak to a doctor and to understand what he was saying. Without her help, Carla could have been in serious trouble.

QUESTION 10.14

Do you take this new story as confirming our formulation or as not confirming it? Explain the basis for your answer.

ANSWER 10.14

The story appears to be strongly confirmatory of our formulation. It speaks of understanding a foreign language which is a common metaphor used to characterize people who understand the strange language of the unconscious mind. It also alludes to two helpful individuals—Marge and the Italian doctor—a sign that the ideas we proposed have been helpful.

Had we missed the key themes and the repressed trigger and offered a less incisive formulation, undoubtedly Carla would have remembered a different incident with Marge, a time when they were on vacation in Canada. Marge was driving and fell asleep at the wheel, and the two women were lucky they hadn't been killed.

Here the themes are of being asleep, not being in touch with reality, not functioning properly, and endangering oneself and others. These are clear signs of error and they would call for a fresh approach to the themes and triggers on hand.

EXERCISE

Take the most recent dream you can remember and engage in guided associating to the dream. Press your associations until they embody some power. Then engage in a trigger search, using the two methods we've identified: conscious listing and using your themes as clues to repressed triggers.

Take the most powerful, currently active trigger you have found and link it to the themes in your pool of themes. Be sure to develop a cause and effect story. Again, the model is: this is what happened; this is how I perceived it; and this is how I unconsciously processed and understood what happened; this is how I reacted to what I experienced; this is what I see should be done about it.

Try also to detect ways in which your unconscious experience has affected your interactions with other people. Strong, disturbing and very real effects stem from these unconscious constellations; look carefully and you'll find them. Typically, they involve emotionally charged choices and decisions or inexplicable actions or feelings you have that don't quite make sense consciously.

> *The effects of unconscious experience are ubiquitous; it continuously influences our behaviors, feelings and lives.*
> *Trigger decoding is the only known antidote to the emotional ills that are built into the evolved design of the human mind.*

If your exercise did not produce a logical story with an unexpected twist and insight, wait until tomorrow and try again with a fresh day of triggers and a fresh dream. To help you with this effort, let's review again the essential steps in the linking process:

1. Build your pool of themes.
2. Discover your *active* triggers.
3. Extract the strongest themes by lifting them from the surface story.

4. Place these extracted themes into contact with the most powerful trigger on hand (using the evident implications of the trigger event as your guide.)

5. Use the trigger and themes to generate a cause and effect statement that begins with your unconscious perceptions and articulates your unconscious experience and your reaction to that experience.

6. Go back to your original surface dream and generate a fresh and new guided association. (If the story has a positive, helpful cast or adds a significant insight into the issues you are working over, your original formulation is probably valid; if the story speaks of error, ignorance, blindness, deafness, and poor functioning, your formulation is likely to have been wrong.)

7. Go back over your triggers and themes to reformulate your thinking if confirmation is lacking. Most often the key to the error is in selecting the wrong trigger event to connect with your themes, so *recheck your triggers first;* if that does not set things straight, then recheck your power themes and try to find a fresh way to link them to your triggers.

This, then, is how we become conscious of our own unconscious experiences. Having dealt almost exclusively with dreams, it's time now to see again how stories of any kind can be trigger decoded to bring us into contact with the same exquisite and powerful world of unconscious experience and wise response.

Chapter 11

The Storied Road to Unconscious Wisdom

As I have said, the unconscious mind speaks to us through stories that encode our unconscious experiences and our processing of these experiences. We have developed the process of trigger decoding using dreams, largely because they are inherently fascinating and easy to recognize and isolate for processing. But as we know, the key issue is not with the dream, but with the *real life* trigger event that provokes the dream. Dreams are but one way of enabling us to reach into our unconscious experience of trigger events.

In contrast with dreams, which we intuitively treat as special communications—(with two layers of meaning)—we tend to think of stories as mundane, single-meaning communications without realizing that they are every bit as special and layered with meaning as are our dreams.

> *Every story we tell or think of, real or imagined, and every story someone else tells us, is, like every dream, a two leveled communication and a means by which we express encoded, unconscious meanings and messages.*

Oddly enough, we generally communicate and experience far more stories than dreams. This means that *stories* and *narratives* are by far the *more common carriers* of encoded messages from the deep unconscious system of our minds. We should learn to pay far more attention to our sto-

163

ries and to make far better use of them as opportunities to reach into the unconscious realm. Doing so requires that we attend to stories first, as direct communications and second, as encoded communications.

> *We must learn to listen to stories with two frames of mind: one that takes the story at face value and the other that struggles to undo the disguise in the same story by extracting its themes and finding its unconscious trigger.*

Two Uses of Stories

There are two ways in which stories can serve us as the carriers of encoded messages.

The Use of Stories as Dream Substitutes There seems to be a natural inclination to work with dreams whenever possible. This is a wise choice because a remembered dream is well casted to carry reactions to many different triggers, all of them waiting to be linked to the dream-associational network you generate through your dream and associations.

There are, however, ways in which stories can play an important role in processing triggers, especially when dreams are either unavailable or not quite getting you to the deep and surprising insights you're searching for.

Make up a story when you don't have a recent dream in hand. If you want to process a particular trigger event or to check out your emotional state and you don't remember a recent dream, all you need to do is make up a short story of any kind that comes to mind. Once the story's been silently told to yourself, you treat it exactly as you would a dream by eliciting guided associations and using the generated pool of themes for linking to your active triggers.

The story you generate should be a product of your *imagination* so it's as close to a dream as possible. This allows the story to be shaped by your *unconscious creative center* in much the same way that the center creates a dream by drawing as it does on conscious and especially unconscious memories, recent events, and your own inner ingenuity.

Introduce a story when dream processing is blocked or unsatisfactory. Whenever your effort to process a dream fails to generate an unexpected trigger decoded insight, you should generate a story and use it as a *supplementary origination narrative.* This story and the fresh guided associations it creates will often get you to the punch lines that had eluded you in working with your dreams.

Introduce a story when you have a very brief dream and are blocked in associating to your dream. Whenever your dream material is thin or not proving to be evocative of powerful guided associations, you should turn to a fresh made-up story and treat it as a waking dream.

To help you develop your imagined stories, these guidelines are relevant:

1. Make certain you are telling a story rather than explaining something or intellectualizing in any way.
2. The story should come from your imagination, whatever else it is based on and you should allow your imagination free reign.
3. Be sure the story is relatively short and that it has a beginning, middle, and end.
4. Allow your story to turn grim if you're so inclined. The stronger the tale, the stronger the associated images, and the more compelling the linked insights are likely to be. However, innocuous stories also have a way of generating strong guided associations, so be sure to associate to the story no matter how thin it may be.

Made-up stories can be thought of as waking dreams and processed accordingly.

THE USE OF STORIES INVOLVING EVERY KIND OF DAILY INTERACTION—THE INTRODUCTION OF MARGINALLY RELATED OR COINCIDENTAL STORIES TOLD IN THE COURSE OF A COMMONPLACE DIALOGUE While we tend to think of ourselves in the flow of a world of conscious experience, it also is true that we are in the flow of a world of unconscious experience as well. Throughout the day, with whomever we come into contact and whatever the situation may be, stories are being told, by ourselves and the other people we are in contact with.

Every story told in any context, situation, or interaction contains some measure of encoded meaning. However, the most powerful carriers of unconscious messages are stories that are not directly related to the interaction or business at hand.

Every narrative carries two messages, one is direct and conscious and the other is indirect and unconscious. However, when a story is told that has a direct bearing on an ongoing discussion, the encoded portion generally is minimal and difficult to detect. For example, if you're telling your child to clean up his room and you tell a tale of how you cleaned your room as a child, there's little room for selective encoded messages. Or if you are trying to sell raw plastics and you tell a story about another customer who profited from using your goods, this is a relatively straightforward tale that would carry little detectable trigger encoded meaning.

The more a story departs from the central discussion on hand, however, the easier it is to automatically incorporate encoded messages into the narrative and to trigger decode them as well.

Here's another brief illustration. Tom and Jane are discussing their children and Jane mentions a problem her friend Kay had with her children that is similar to one they are facing with their own. The story of the friend's problem, while it carries encoded meaning, is directly relevant to the conscious issue the couple is facing. In thinking through the meaning of the story, this conscious function, designed to clarify a real problem under direct discussion, is likely to capture almost all of the detectable meaning in the narrative.

The only room for encoding would be in the nature of the friend's problem, but the more it resembles the one facing Tom and Jane, the less it serves as a carrier of encoded meaning. Still, any departure from the specific topic under discussion would indicate that the story has a notable trigger encoded meaning.

While they're talking, Tom suddenly mentions a television play he'd seen. "Oh by the way," he begins, "that show you missed really upset me. It was about a woman who had a high-level job and began to neglect her children to the point where one of them nearly overdosed on drugs."

Given that Tom and Jane's two children are two and four years old respectively, this last story is not directly relevant to their discussion. As a marginally related story, it must be a carrier of important encoded messages.

QUESTION 11.1

Can you identify the trigger for this coincidental story and suggest its possible decoded meaning?

ANSWER 11.1

The trigger event is the *immediate* discussion between Tom and Jane, and for Tom, who told the story, it's Jane's part of their conversation. A secondary trigger is the problem with their children. More specifically, as Jane was quick to realize, the story encodes Tom's impression that Jane's having a job is accountable for the problems they're having with their children.

Marginally related stories generally stand by themselves and seldom evoke further guided associations. But we have a great advantage in processing them for trigger decoded meaning because they are composed on the spot, at the very moment of an emotionally charged exchange with another person. They are an instantaneous unconsciously driven reaction to an ongoing and immediate trigger experience. The primary trigger event for these coincidental stories is always known and readily available for linking to the themes of the marginally related story.

Made-up stories reveal the rapidity with which the deep unconscious system processes trigger events and their implications; no sooner is the trigger conveyed than a response is made.

Let's spell this out in the form of some principles:

1. *Unconscious perception and communication is everywhere and continuously active.* Encoded expression is inherent to human language and to all narratives. Unconscious experience is continuous and exists even when we are engaged in our daily chores, or engaged in our most common interactions, whether they are in business, family, education or any other daily occurrences.

It is a mistake to believe that unconscious experience is limited to a special class of emotionally charged relationships, such as those we have with loved ones. There is an emotional side to virtually every notable event in our lives. Unconscious experience plays an extremely significant, however unrecognized, role in how we function, relate, live, and thrive, or suffer.

2. On the whole, story lines are easy to recognize. The key to being able to harness the unconscious meanings of a story lies first and foremost with recognizing that a story has both surface and encoded meaning. This entails a shift into an unusual mode of thinking for everyday discourse, a dual mode in which you hear and understand the surface story, yet at the same time, you realize there's a displaced, disguised story being told as well.

In essence, then, to trigger decode a marginally related story, you need to consciously realize that an encoded story has just been communicated.

3. In the course of everyday life, our minds are designed to fix our listening and thinking at the surface, survival-related level of experience. It is quite unnatural for us to think that there is also an encoded message in what is being said because this requires an entirely different way of thinking.

While survival communication must be direct and to the point, unconscious communication must be indirect and away from the point. In this second way of operating, we must listen to a story as a disguised message. We must treat its themes as belonging to another context or scene, to a trigger far different from the context of the direct story.

> *The story that is being told with a conscious purpose also is being told for an unconscious purpose. To fathom this second purpose, we must not take the story at face value, but must reach toward unmasking its disguises.*

4. The main trigger for a marginally related story is the relationship with the person to whom the story is being told—the immediate situation and interaction. This means that as soon as you hear a coincidental story, you can have in mind the unconscious trigger for the story. You can then quickly engage in the linking process and trigger decoding.

5. As always, the linking of the themes in the story to the trigger situation should be cast in the form of defining the actual unconscious experience of the story teller. It is helpful to have a sense of the implications of the trigger situation—the nature of your relationship with the other person—regardless of who tells the story. This will guide your extraction of themes and your connecting them to the immediate experience.

6. It is a good rule to *avoid story telling of your own* when an interaction is charged and important to you, even in business. The problem with a marginally-related story is that it reveals an enormous amount of information about yourself and your perceptions of the other person that is unconsciously sent and unconsciously received. The effects of the story are strong yet

unknown to either yourself or the other person. Many strange, inexplicable, and puzzling things happen in human interactions because of these unrecognized unconscious communications. Let the story teller beware!

7. When another person tells a marginally related story, recognize it for what it is. As you continue to talk and interact with that person, try to think about your relationship with them and what is happening at the moment between you. Take the themes of their story, extract them from the story as told, and bring them into linkage with the trigger situation of the moment.

Formulating the resultant trigger decoded message will give you a sense of how the other person unconsciously is experiencing what you've done and said—including otherwise hidden issues. This provides you with invaluable information that can direct your subsequent comments and actions.

8. Decode another person's coincidental story *with all due caution* and try to confirm your impressions through a quick story of your own—told to yourself, however. If the other person tells another story, it also should confirm in some disguised way your reading of the earlier storied communication. *Make every effort to validate your impressions.*

9. Do not tell the other person your understanding of their unconscious messages. These messages are unconscious because the other person does not want to know what they are. Decoding a story for them is experienced as an assault. In addition, this kind of decoding has a high risk

of error and you can look very foolish if you've missed something or are wrong. Under these circumstances, trigger decoding is a side effort and bringing it into the direct line of engagement with another person is off-putting. Keep your knowledge to yourself and use it wisely.

In all, marginally related stories are relatively easy to decode because the trigger is readily identified and the images and their themes tend to link easily to the trigger event. The pool of themes is not cluttered with themes from guided associations so the thematic part is also readily handled.

Let's extend these explorations of marginally related stories with a fresh exercise.

EXERCISE

George is offering to sell large quantities of raw materials to Alan, who is vice-president of a manufacturing company. George mentions that there are ways to sweeten the deal for Alan if he gives the green light to go forward with the terms that George is offering him. It can be done so no one will ever know what went down, adds George.

Alan seems to ignore George's comment and asks some questions about the quality of the steel George intends to deliver. As George is responding, Alan interrupts. "You want to hear something really weird?" he asks, "We found out that one of the men in our plant was stealing rods of steel and selling them to bootleg gun manufacturers. Talk about horrors; we turned him over to the police. He'll never work for us again. He should have known better than to get involved with ruthless people like that."

QUESTION 11.2

Where is the marginally related story is this anecdote?
Who tells it and what are its main themes?

ANSWER 11.2

Alan's story of the worker who stole the steel is a marginally related or coincidental story. It has its logic as part of the discussion of the steel he might buy from George, but it is not directly related to the negotiations at hand. It would be easy to take the story for granted as an interesting and sad addendum to what is going on between the two men; most people would do no more than that. But we've been alerted to the fact that these narratives carry a second, encoded message, so let's pursue the unconscious communication disguised in this story.

QUESTION 11.3

What is the trigger for this marginally related story? In answering, identify the general trigger situation, but then specify the exact communication that unconsciously evoked this story from Alan.

ANSWER 11.3

The general trigger situation is the interaction and dialogue between Alan and George. The definitive trigger within that situation is George's hint that Alan could expect a kick-back or pay-off if he bought the materials from George.

QUESTION 11.4

What are the main attributes of this triggering communication? Characterize them in terms of *themes*.

ANSWER 11.4

The trigger's most powerful attribute is that of dishonesty and criminality. There is also an implication of collusion and secretiveness, and of course, the illicit passage of money from one person to another.

QUESTION 11.5

What are the main *themes* in the story Alan told? Which of these themes are *bridging themes* that extend from the surface story to an encoded description of the trigger?

The main *themes* in Alan's story are those of thievery, dishonesty, illegal and illicit collusion, and being caught and sent to jail. The *bridging themes* are those of criminality and collusion.

QUESTION 11.6

The encoded story reflects Alan's unconscious processing of George's offer. Consciously, Alan was uncertain as to what he should do; he was tempted to take the pay-off because he needed money desperately, but concerned lest there be a slip-up and he'd get caught. Everyone does it, he rationalized, but some people get caught, he countered. Even as he gave off his encoded response, consciously he was debating the offer but coming to no conclusion.

While he waffled consciously, unconsciously Alan was very clear as to his answer. In his deep unconscious mind he knew for certain that he was being asked to do something dishonest and criminal, there were no excuses or false qualifiers there.

While consciously uncertain what to do, what was Alan's unconscious recommendation to himself, his adaptive solution to George's offer?

ANSWER 11.6

Turning the dishonest employee over to the police and stating that he'd never work for them again indicates that Alan was aware of the criminal act he was being asked to get involved in. By reminding himself that people go to jail for crimes like that, Alan was telling himself to not accept the bribe. He affirms this position when he remarks that his employee should have known better than to get involved with dishonest people like that.

Alan knew enough about trigger decoding to realize that he had told a marginally related story and it was relatively easy for him to trigger decode his unconscious messages to both George and himself. He decided not to accept George's offer and to not do business with him. George was unscrupulous and couldn't be trusted. Soon after telling his story, Alan sent George packing.

Notice too that if George had consciously recognized Alan's story as an encoded communication (unconsciously, there is no doubt that he heard the encoded message in Alan's tale), he quickly could have changed his approach to the situation. Whether this would have affected Alan's decision not to do business with George is an open question, but that shift was the only hope George had to set things back on course.

Finally, it is well to realize that a major *frame violation* was at issue here. Consciously, Alan was unable to take a clear stand for a secured frame and refute the proposed frame violation, an illegal act and violation of the law. On the other hand, his deep unconscious mind zeroed in on the frame break as a violation of the law, pure and simple. His deep mind quickly and unmistakably spoke for the secured frame, the decision to stay within the law.

> *This is, as previously mentioned, quite characteristic of how the two systems of the mind react to frame-related issues: the conscious system generally is inclined toward frame alterations and the deep unconscious system is totally committed to securing frames.*

Life is filled with marginally related stories. Whoever you are and whatever shifting roles you occupy, the people you meet and interact with will tell you coincidental stories and you are likely to tell a few such stories to them yourself. We all communicate both conscious and unconscious messages to each other day in and day out.

However, the adaptive advantage—the stronger coping capacity—goes to those who know how to trigger decode these narrative tales.

Once again, make the day ahead one in which you will be on the alert for marginally related stories, your own as well as those from others. Listen carefully for the emergence of a narrative, especially when the going gets rough. Understand that whenever you get into an immutable circular argument in which you and the other person simply disagree and can't see each other's position, you can be certain that there's a hidden unconscious issue fueling the dispute. The same applies to situations in which you are trying to show someone the obvious error of their ways and they just can't see it.

In all such instances, the person who tells the first coincidental story will encode the unconscious issue that needs to be resolved before the conscious dispute can be settled. Listen carefully and wisely, and be sure to look for the underlying issue and trigger decode the themes of the story in light of the deeper trigger. Often, the themes of the story will point you to a specific trigger you had missed— these methods have a lot to offer.

There are many everyday signs of unconscious influence. Arguments at an impasse, fixed but inappropriate ways of thinking or behaving, feeling anxious or depressed for reasons that escape you, sensing something is amiss even though you can't get quite find out what it is, having intrusive or impulsive or inappropriate thoughts, and the like. In all such situations the only possible way to truly resolve the problem is through trigger decoding.

Be on the lookout for difficulties of this kind. And keep your ears open for a coincidental story that will illuminate the specific unconscious issues that are involved. Listen to the story for *correctives* and *guidelines* as to how the underlying situation should be dealt with. Use your knowledge of trigger decoding to give yourself and those around you a far better chance at living their lives healthy and well.

EXERCISE

Here's a final exercise. Sue is Diane's mother; Diane is a teenager. Whatever Sue asks Diane to do—straighten up her room, wash the dishes, be home before 11 P.M., finish her homework before going out or before getting on the phone—Diane just doesn't do it. She's full of excuses and is driving her mother to distraction.

They sit down to discuss the problem. It never used to be this way, Sue reminds her daughter. Sue spells out the issues as clearly as she can and Diane simply comes up with new excuses. But in the middle of these going-nowhere exchanges, Diane says she's got to call Pat who's been real upset the last two days.

It seems that Pat's parents took away her driving privileges because she had taken their car without permission. They also put her on a curfew so she's not allowed out after 6 P.M. "It's not right for her parents to take away her freedom like that," Diane commented, "she's grown up now and should be free to come and go as she likes, as long as it's within reason. She should be allowed to be responsible for her choices and not have them dictated to her by her parents."

Identify the main themes in this marginally related story. On that basis, try to suggest a trigger or two that could have evoked these themes.

ANSWER 11.8

The main themes are acting against rules and being punished for it through parental restrictions, being confined, and the corrective suggestion to allow for freedom of choice within reason and for responsibility for one's own decisions and life.

At first thought, the trigger may seem to be the consciously acknowledged effort by Sue to discipline her daughter and have her conform to a set of obligations. But this trigger would not call for a coincidental story and for unconscious processing unless there was another, hidden issue involved.

There was, in fact, another issue. It was not mentioned by daughter or mother, and they didn't think of it while they were talking. The problem had gone underground and was affecting both of them outside of their respective conscious thinking and experience. It was the kind of unconscious issue that fuels these kinds of unresolvable problems between parents and their children.

About a month earlier, around the time Diane began to become so recalcitrant, her parents had discovered that secretly, Diane was dating a boy who was of a different religion from hers. Angered by their daughter's secrecy and by the religious differences, Diane's parents had forbidden her to see the boy again. Diane objected for a while and then dropped the issue. She had seen the boy in school a few times and felt that she had lost interest in him.

What the conscious mind drops, the unconscious mind often will persist in dealing with.

QUESTION 11.9

In Diane's story, what are the *bridging themes* that link the narrative to the trigger event? And what is her unconscious adaptive suggestion? How does she propose that the situation be resolved?

ANSWER 11.9

The *bridging themes* are doing something behind the backs of one's parents, and without parental permission, and being punished and constrained in response to it. The adaptive suggestion is for the parents to allow their child freedom of choice within reason.

Sue picked up Diane's story as an encoded message and was jarred into remembering what had happened a month earlier. She decided to bring up this underlying issue and despite Diane's claim that it didn't bother her, Sue said she'd discuss the problem with Diane's father. She suggested that the three of them should sit down and rework the problem in order to come to a better solution and with a little thought and discussion, she was sure they would change their position.

It should not surprise you that Diane soon went back to being her old neat and reasonably cooperative self again, which was her own and her mother's reward for Sue's ability to trigger decode her daughter's marginally related story.

SOME FINAL COMMENTS

We are, as a species, so fixed in our conscious ways of thinking and coping, it is only with great difficulty that we come to realize that we live a *second life* embedded in the *first, conscious one*.

Historically, the major dream interpreters, beginning with Freud and Jung, and extending into the many present day practitioners and writers, all traded in insights that belong to our conscious world of experience. These are easy insights and no matter how hard we try to dress them up, they're not all that important for the course of our lives. There is a far more powerful system of communication and mental activity buried beneath that more superficial realm.

The distinctive features of trigger decoding and of the deeply unconscious world of experience are difficult to appreciate, as is the world they outline. We don't cope well with worlds that we experience only indirectly and through a decoding procedure. But that world is real, as real as the deep system of the mind that operates within its domain.

The human mind has a most unexpected and peculiar structure with far too much out of conscious reach. We have taken this journey together in order to develop the tools and skills with which to explore this world beyond awareness and to benefit from the deep wisdom that pervades its kingdom. You are well advised to use these skills often and with perserverance; they are certain to give you a remarkable body of insights into the emotional sphere, more satisfying relationships, and a fuller, happier, more successful life.

Index